Desiring Theology

Boris Luchanski   1/600

Religion & Postmodernism
A Series Edited by Mark C. Taylor

DESIRING THEOLOGY

Charles E. Winquist

University of Chicago Press
Chicago & London

Charles E. Winquist is the Thomas J. Watson Professor of Religion
at Syracuse University and the author of numerous books, including, more recently, *Epiphanies of Darkness: Deconstruction in
Theology* (1986).

The University of Chicago Press, Chicago 60637
The University of Chicago Press, Ltd., London
© 1995 by The University of Chicago
All rights reserved. Published 1995
Printed in the United States of America
04 03 02 01 00 99 98 97 96 95   1 2 3 4 5

ISBN: 0–226–90212–9 (cloth)
          0–226–90213–7 (paper)

Library of Congress Cataloging-in-Publication Data

Winquist, Charles E., 1944–
    Desiring theology / Charles E. Winquist.
        p.   cm. — (Religion and postmodernism)
    Includes bibliographical references and index.
    1. Theology—History—20th century. 2. Philosophy, Modern—20th
century. 3. Deconstruction. 4. Postmodernism. 5. Postmodernism—
Religious aspects—Christianity. I. Title. II. Series.
BT28.W584   1995
230′.01—dc20   94–20218
                                                                                      CIP

♾ The paper used in this publication meets the minimum requirements of
the American National Standard for Information Sciences—Permanence of
Paper for Printed Library Materials, ANSI Z39.48-1984.

Frontispiece: Boris Luchanski, *A girl with a doll.* Courtesy the artist.
Photograph: Courtney Frisse.

Contents

For
my mother
June Winquist
and
my daughter
Heidi Erika Winquist

Preface

In a remarkable sermon, entitled "The Depth of Existence," Paul Tillich, through a series of disturbing questions, suggests that the desire for truth is related to a profound disappointment with the surfaces of experience and an expectation "that the truth which does not disappoint dwells below the surfaces in the depth."[1] Tillich understands "depth" to be a symbol for a spiritual quality in life. This sermon, although published in 1948, continues to persuade us to consider that at the end of the twentieth century there is still a desire for a thinking which does not disappoint. Since the time of that sermon there have been a number of paradigmatic shifts in philosophical thinking that make it questionable whether we can simply fold Tillich's language into contemporary discourse and proceed with what he called "my search for absolutes."[2] We now live in a postmodern age without absolutes, and the ontotheological frame of Tillich's theology has been questioned and challenged by postmodern theories of discourse formation and deconstructive philosophies.

In the following pages I have equated the desire for a thinking which does not disappoint with a desire to think theologically. There is a restlessness and an anxiety when we live only with traces of religion and outside of a sphere of meaning and discourse that gives

1. Paul Tillich, *The Shaking of the Foundations* (New York: Charles Scribner's Sons, 1948) p. 53.
2. Paul Tillich, *My Search for Absolutes* (New York: Simon and Schuster, 1967).

importance to life. The notion of "depth" articulated by Tillich is a valuation of experience which requires reconfiguration to be credible in the context of postmodern secular thinking. I will suggest that to seek depth today is to desire a complex association of meanings that are weighted with a sense of being real and important. This is a desire to know an "other" in and of language that can be valued in the forming of personal and communal identity. This is a desire to think the singularities of experience that can exfoliate themselves in the production of new meaning. What remains of Tillich's formulation of depth is the desire for a thinking that resists the trivialization of ultimate questions. There is in this formulation a secular mandate for theology even in the context of the transitoriness, contingency, and dissimulations of postmodern thinking.

There is yet another meaning of desiring theology. This is the understanding that theology written in the wake of psychoanalysis and all of its intellectual entailments must elaborate the meaning and importance of desire in its own discourse. The Lacanian rereading of Freud in relationship to the orders of the real, the imaginary, and the symbolic confronts us with the problem of accessing the meaning of desire even over against the sedimentation of language. What is special about theology as a discursive practice is that its extreme formulations are intensive uses of language that can and often do transgress the repressive totalizations of dominant discourses. Texts are fissured so that they are not immune to their context in life, which includes primary forces of desire. Theology accesses forces that must be articulated in its own elaboration if it is to be adequate to the meaning of its experience. To desire theological thinking is soon implicated in thinking the meaning of desire. Accessing forces exceeds and transgresses the representational economy of thinking, giving significance to meaning. I am suggesting that we find life more rich and satisfying in this complexity.

The opening studies in this book are theoretical and generally philosophical. The construction of the self as subjectivity by Descartes and its further elaboration by Kant are explored in relationship to assessing the limits and possibilities of transcendental philosophy as a resource for understanding the possibilities for a theological discursive practice. Transgressing these limits is to deconstruct the transcendental philosophy of the subject and transform it into a more modest provisional transcendental inquiry into the possibilities for meaningful discourse, and I draw extensively from the philosophical works of Nietzsche, Gilles Deleuze, and Jacques Derrida in formulating this transformation. If thinking has a heterological infrastructure and no point of absolute reference, what does it mean to think theologically? What is theological text production?

To substantively address these questions, I enter into conversations with the profoundly Christian theologies of Paul Tillich and Robert P. Scharlemann and the a/theological writings of Mark C. Taylor. How does the name of God, the word of God, or the death of God alter thinking and its discursive expression? Can theology help us think beyond the dominance of subjectivity? Conversations with these subtle and complex theological voices help delineate an agenda for desiring theology.

This agenda is pragmatic as well as theoretical. First, in a secular culture there is no simple proper domain for theological thinking. Tactically, I suggest at the close of this book that theology is closely akin to what Gilles Deleuze and Felix Guattari refer to as a minor intensive use of a major language.[3] Second, theology is a minor literature in the dominant community, but it also transforms the meaning of community. Within the dominant community there is a desiring community that makes concrete a vision of finitude that is beyond despair. The minor intensive theological use of language pressures the ordinary weave of discourse and opens it to desire. Meaning is intensified. Theology is a work against the disappointment of thinking.

While writing this book I was often privileged to be in intensive communities and to participate in conversations that significantly contributed to my theological understanding. There are several of my colleagues at Syracuse University that I particularly want to thank

---

3. Gilles Deleuze and Felix Guattari, *Kafka: Toward a Minor Literature*, translated by Dana Polan (Minneapolis: University of Minnesota Press, 1986) pp. 16–27.

for their support. Alan Berger, David L. Miller, Patricia Cox Miller, and James Wiggins have been generous with their encouragement, insights, and criticism, as have my former colleagues at Syracuse University, Charles H. Long and Susan Shapiro. I also want to acknowledge the importance of the friendship and ongoing theological conversations with Thomas J. J. Altizer, Robert P. Scharlemann, and Mark C. Taylor.

There are many students at Syracuse University to whom I am indebted. I particularly want to mention Victor Taylor of the Humanities Doctoral Program and Noëlle Vahanian of the Religion Department because they read the manuscript, critiqued my ideas, and encouraged me throughout the development of this book.

There are also institutions that have supported me and provided spaces for the critical engagement with ideas developed in this book. Syracuse University has been my home during the development of this book and has also supported me on a research leave to Greece at an important time in the development of my thinking. I have also been privileged to give lectures and enter into conversations during formative stages of this book at the University of Colorado, the University of Toronto, the University of Cambridge, the Aristotle University of Thessaloniki, and the II and III International Paul Tillich Symposia in Frankfurt am Main, Germany.

Much of this book was written during several extended visits to Greece, and I want to thank the Fulbright Educational Foundation of Greece for the support they provided to me and the assistance and friendship of William [Chip] Ammerman and George Dariotis of Athens and Demetri Doutis of Thessaloniki. I am especially indebted to Anastasia Lymperiadou for her kindness, friendship, and hospitality during my visits to Thessaloniki.

One

The Exigency of Theological Thinking

Even if they belong to some religious sect, people need to open up to the unknown—let it come in and stir things up! We also need to open up the law and leave it open, so that something can come in and upset the usual mechanisms of liberty. We need to open to what's impious and what's forbidden, so that the unknown element in things may enter and be seen.

Marguerite Duras, *Practicalities*

For whom am I writing? Who are those people who want life to be at least slightly disturbed by life's possibilities? These are people that have at least some fascination with the unknown element in things. They are not the cultured despisers of religion although they are usually cultured. Sometimes they were raised in religious traditions and may have at one time been active in formal institutional religious life. Or, especially among younger readers, their experiences of growing up may have been fully secular with the institutions of religious traditions only marginally impinging upon them. Their education appears to have made religion irrelevant to their lives, although they may be curious about its trappings in much the same way a tourist is interested in visiting cathedrals on a European holiday or Shinto temples while in Japan.

The dominant culture in Europe and North America is secular and the readers that I envision for this book are deeply influenced by this culture. They would almost never read theology, but they might approach its periphery through interests in the arts, literature, depth psychologies, or even various "New Age" spiritualities.

Those for whom I write are restless. They have noted an absence in their lives, but it is not an absence that can be readily filled by institutionalized religion. Their experience parallels Carl Jung's insight that once the gods have left the temples they never return or, for those who grew up in a fully secular milieu, there never were recognizable goddesses or gods in the temple. They live only with traces of religion in their personal or collective memories. Sometimes there is a residual resistance to religion but, more commonly, there is only a benign neglect of at least the institutions of religion.

The sense of absence is not associated with being outside of religious institutions but is instead experienced as feeling outside a sphere of meaning and discourse that gives importance to life. What is noticed is the trivializing of both life's passages and the talk about these passages. It is not that there is a vast loss of meaning, but patterns of meaning have come to lack intensity and importance. The dissemination of meaning in an age of global communication and media saturation has too often been a diminishment of significance. We are crowded, sometimes overwhelmed, by meanings that float on the surface of consciousness.

Religious questions arise even if we don't trust traditional answers. Is this all there is? Can the surfaces of experiences give way to depths or can we reach heights and thereby transform the ordinariness of life? Can there be, at the end and turn of the twentieth century, a credible *apologia* for religious life? Is the human capacity for the production of religious meanings more than a form of obscurantism?

These questions are not new to our time. At the beginning of the nineteenth century, Friedrich Schleiermacher published his *On Religion: Speeches to Its Cultured Despisers*.[1] He appealed to the immediacy of experience to develop an understanding of religion that did not require a prior commitment of faith or investment in church doctrine and institutional structures. He asked his educated readers to suspend their suspicions of religion, which he thought were fundamentally directed toward the trappings of religion and not against religion itself.

The well-known definitions of religious experience as the feeling of absolute dependence and the contemplation of pious life as lived so that the finite is experienced in and through the infinite, the tem-

---

1. Friedrich Schleiermacher, *On Religion: Speeches to Its Cultured Despisers,* translated by John Oman (New York: Harper Torchbooks, 1958). Further page references are cited in the text.

poral in and through the eternal, are rooted in a humanist understanding of subjectivity (pp. 36, 49–50). His appeal to experience,
attractive even at the end of the twentieth century, presupposes a
unity of experience and the singleness of the human subject.
It is this presupposition of a unified subject and the accompanying assertion of the dominance of subjectivity that is suspicious at the
end of the twentieth century. It is this presupposition that has problematized Schleiermacher's understanding of religion as an appeal to
immediate experience.

I mention Schleiermacher at the beginning of this chapter
because I want to begin with his project and its appeal to immediate
experience in the understanding of religion. The importance of
Schleiermacher, aside from his being a parent of so much modern liberal theology, is that his understanding of religion is also an exploration of a depth dimension to human existence that is missing in the
testimony of much of secular culture.

Schleiermacher affirms that we are born with a religious capacity.
"If only his sense for the profoundest depths of his own nature is not
crushed out, if only all fellowship between himself and the Primal
Source is not quite shut off, religion would, after its own fashion,
infallibly be developed" (p. 124). It is religion that raises the simple
melody of the individual calling of life to a "full-voiced, glorious harmony" (p. 89).

It is the infusion of life with meaning, thus transforming the
ordinariness of events from a brute dreariness, that is the promise of
Schleiermacher's formulations concerning religion. If this promise
has credibility, the achievement of a secularized culture liberating the
human condition from the strictures of religious life appears ironically also as a liberation from meaningfulness. Those of us who have
identified with the dominant secular culture also have a vague sense
of not experiencing finite existence in and through the infinite. It is
even hard to think what such a formulation might mean. It is not
surprising that this sense of lack is usually not brought to full articulation but is instead felt as a nostalgia for lost meanings commonly
associated with childhood memories of a time of fullness, even if this
time is a retrospective construction outside of any lived time.

What we have come to experience is that, except for discursive ruminations of a lost paradise that is always a dim memory and somewhat loose construction, we do not have a discourse that is weighted with complex associations of meanings experienced as both real and important. It is this absence that suggests a more modest beginning than that of Schleiermacher.

Very few of us in the secular world can or have borne witness to having experiences of finite things against a horizon of the infinite. We may be awed by the bigness of some finite things and by the ability to push concepts to dimensions of incomprehensibility, but this awe is only an approximation of Schleiermacher's feeling of absolute dependence. Schleiermacher constructed a definition of religion out of an experience that most of us have not had. Instead of being inclusive of what we might call religion, it now functions negatively, excluding experiences that cannot meet its measure.

The more modest definition that I propose is that religion can be indexed in the flux of life by what we value as real and important. There is a redundancy in this definition since the sense of what is real is determined by its sense of importance. I maintain the word *real* to keep our inquiry bound to specific and concrete experience in the production of discourse. There is a parallel concern in my minimal definition with Tillich's understanding of religion as the depth dimension of culture, but it does not go as far as Tillich to mark the criteria for theology as a matter of ultimate concern and a matter of being and not being.[2] A postmodern theology cannot begin in sanctuaries where there is, as a presupposition, a witness of faith, although these sanctuaries can be visited. Theology can look for or try to construct a depth dimension to culture, but it cannot assume with any credibility that there is in any natural reality such a depth.

The notion of depth is a valuation of experiences and the real question is whether such a value can be assigned to any experience or complex of experiences in our secular culture. Surely, Schleierma-

2. Paul Tillich, *Systematic Theology*, 3 vols. (Chicago: University of Chicago Press, 1951, 1957, 1963), vol. 1:12, 14.

cher's feeling of absolute dependence or Tillich's ultimate concern would qualify for a valuation of depth if we had such experiences. Traditional concepts of revelation cloaked in numinosity would qualify if we had such experiences. A secular postmodern theology begins with an acknowledgment of a lack of such experiences in many of our lives and asks if any experience can be had or so transformed such that it can be valued as real and important.

Is it as simple as Schleiermacher suggests? Will religion develop infallibly if we only learn how to not snuff out the sense of the profoundest depths? This is a labyrinthine problem because, if we do not have a sense of the profoundest depths, it is hard to locate where and how this sense is repressed.

There are witnesses in our collective historical memory that claim that they have had this experience of the profoundest depths and if we are to hear their voices we will need to intersect their discourses in ways that are both meaningful and credible for us. Their discourses will have to become valenced with our discourse if they are to provide access to religious experience. This means that we will first have to locate in our own experiences those places or moments which can connect with their witness. Otherwise, their witness will be no more than a curiosity for us. The trust in pious teachers has been sufficiently diminished that exhortations to piety are not enough. It is not a question of whether we should have or want to have religious experiences but whether we can have such experiences.

A significant complication in lifting the repression of our religious capacity is that in the twentieth century it is often thought that religion and especially its institutions are themselves sources of repression. The symptoms of repression can be sufficiently confused so that Schleiermacher's lifting of repression is not a straightforward matter.

An important quality of the unconscious, unthought, and unsaid is the negation of presence. They are out of mind. Symptomatic presence is a substitution so that what is present is something that is something else. This gives the peculiar feeling that religious life is always elsewhere. This is even a stipulation in theologies where ultimate reality is conceived of as wholly other. This is the production of a nonconcept that eludes even metaphorical expansion unless the integrity of the formulation is violated.

We are at one of those intersections where the demand or desire for religious life is in conflict with the formulation of basic concepts that are regulative of discourse concerning religious life. In a secular milieu, traditional theological formulations block access to religious life by their dislocation from what appears to be ordinary patterns of discourse. The irony is that conceptual formulations that protect an investment in religious life also prohibit an investment in religious life for those who are not already in a community of faith unless they radically can be reconceived.

During more optimistic epochs of enlightenment rationalism, humanism, and romanticism, the self-exclusion of religion by its own theological formulations might have seemed a gratuitous development further isolating the repressive aspects of religious life from the fulfillment of the human promise. In the twentieth century, this promise in all of its many expressions seems false and not capable of fulfillment on its own terms. The self confidence in rationality and individual fulfillment has lost its mooring, especially for those who were highly conscious of rational and individual goals. What seemed deep was another surface that when rationalized was disappointing and sometimes dangerous. Utopian expectations were not salvific when experienced over against the many epiphanies of darkness that have characterized the modern experience of history.

Not only has the twentieth century magnified the horrors of totalitarianism by its technological achievements (now even continued existence on the earth is threatened by nuclear or ecological apocalypse), but as we have been told by Milan Kundera—and before him by Nietzsche—our very sense of reality has become unbearably light. Like Kundera's fictional character Sabina, our lot is "not the burden but the unbearable lightness of being."[3]

We have experienced a progressive series of losses that has left us

3. Milan Kundera, *The Unbearable Lightness of Being*, translated by Michael Heim (New York: Harper & Row, 1984), p. 122.

in a world of contingency and relativity. We are never able to say of any value or experience, "it must be," because we are aware that it could just as well be otherwise. The death of God and the disappearance of a unified and single subject as legacies of the nineteenth century are perhaps the most vivid of our losses, although they entail other losses, such as the end of the meaning of history and the closure of the book as a source of wisdom.[4]

There is still an experience of necessity, but it is blind. That is, events and things are what they are and they cannot be otherwise now that they are what they are. But, the most radical expression of contingency is the contingency of this necessity. The necessity of things as they are, the incorrigibility of fact, does not deny that it could have been otherwise or affirm that this is the best possible world. It simply marks the place where we must begin an interrogation of life.

There should be a probity in our thinking that guards against an epistemological and metaphysical voluntarism that doesn't like the way the world manifests itself and therefore decides to know or construct the world as a wish fulfillment. The incorrigibility of fact will be like a return of the repressed for voluntaristic constructions of the world. The failures of humanisms and romantic idealisms in their utopian projects are examples of the inability to deny forces that subverted their dreams. Voluntarisms are not just free plays of the imagination that reside in no place, a utopian space. They are repressions.

If theology is to accept a construct of religion as being about what is real and important in life, then it must seek an honesty in its own reflections that acknowledges its beginning in the middle of experience. In the middle of experience, theology will be buffeted about by the forces of incorrigibility that act upon it. This is not only its beginning but it is also its task.

4. See Mark Taylor, *Erring: A Postmodern A/theology* (Chicago: University of Chicago Press, 1984), part one.

Two

Beginnings

> Let us begin by accepting the notion that although there is an irre-
> ducible subjective core to human experience, this experience is also his-
> torical and secular, it is accessible to analysis and interpretation, and—
> centrally important—it is not exhausted by totalizing theories, not
> marked and limited by doctrinal or national lines, not confined once
> and for all to analytical constructs.
>
> Edward W. Said, *Culture and Imperialism*

Beginnings cannot assume the possibility of unmediated experience. To begin in the middle is to accept that beginnings are
always already crowded with images, ideologies, histories, fictions,
literatures, and other diverse discursive practices; and, at the same
time, crowded with bodies, rocks, crystals, dogs, and other pressures of organic and inorganic flux. The entanglements of nature,
history, and culture dispel any illusions of a conceptual purity based
in exclusive appeals to nature, history, or culture. There is no knowledge of nature or history uncontaminated by the ideological imagination and there is no free play of culture uncontaminated by natural forces and historical events. Fantasies of purity of thought,
univocal and unambiguous languages, or unmediated experiences
are sullied by interference from the other of exclusion. The methodological dilemma is not where to begin (we have to begin in the
middle of experience), but how do we begin an interrogation of this
experience as to what we can value as real and important?

Because of the heterogeneity of middling experience, there will
already be some privileging of certain experiences by how we gather
them to be placed under interrogation. Collection is an interpretive
act and it, like the experience under investigation, will have a
genealogical and natural history. Even the conditions of assent to
intelligibility in the collection of experience will have a genealogical
and natural history subject to already-formed values and diverse

forces, many of which have not come into consciousness but are conditions of consciousness. Both the privilege of consciousness and the privileging of consciousness are at the heart of our dilemma of beginning. However we start, our beginning is tentative and heuristic. It is an anticipation of an intelligibility that is to be produced. Beginning is a strategic choice. It makes a difference how we imagine this choice. Modern philosophy begins with a radical strategy. It begins with a search for roots or foundations of knowledge. The image of the root, the radix, of consciousness was a severe image of a taproot from which a tree of knowledge could spread. Rigorous methods of exclusion were developed to purify reason and thinking of the confused and ambiguous presentation of experience as given.

Paradigmatic of this strategy and a significant turn to the dominance of subjectivity in defining the philosophical project is *The Meditations Concerning First Philosophy* by Descartes.[1] In his first meditation, he explains how he conceived of his project. He thought that he was at a time in his life in which he would be at fault if he did not interrogate the foundations of his knowledge (p. 75). Using a tool of radical doubt, in which he would exclude any knowledge that was not clear and distinct in its certainty, he was able in the first day of meditation to dismiss the whole phantasmagoria of the world of experience and even suspend judgment on his own existence (pp. 75–80).

Privileging the discourse of radical doubt left him with its only product: subjectivity, which he affirmed in the second of his meditations. "I must finally conclude and maintain that this proposition: *I am, I exist*, is necessarily true every time that I pronounce it or conceive it in my mind" (p. 82). On subsequent days, subjectivity was now free to construct a world and a god with the single reference and principle of intelligibility being itself. The philosopher could then discover the subjective foundations of knowledge by examining the world that was reconstructed out of the discourse of the subject.

---

1. René Descartes, *Discourse on Method and Meditations*, translated by Laurence J. Lafleur (Indianapolis: Bobbs-Merrill, 1960). Further page references will be cited in the text.

Meaning, clarity, and truth all became the domain of the subject. A reversal into modernity occurred in this move. Inner reality was valued over the external world.

A coin of subjectivity was minted in the forge of Descartes's *Meditations* which was to become the dominant currency of the Enlightenment and the culture developed from it. As that coin was traded and the marks of its origin were effaced, it was thought to be natural and the way things are. The inner reality of the subject and the privileging of consciousness became the truth of the self even while the figures of subjectivity underwent many permutations in various empiricisms, idealisms, romanticisms, and even existentialisms. Reality was construed not just as what is present but as what is present to consciousness. Subjectivity was the source and arbiter of reality. This affirmation is what gave a preeminence to the individual in the ethos of public life and has in some ways obscured the meaning and importance of community.

Private life was shrouded in the truth of subjectivity. The irony of subjectivity being the arbiter of reality is that in order to have a world that can be maintained within the prescriptions of its order, the world would have to be other than itself in a substitute system of subjective signification. Language is a first order of substitution. Then, the priority of signifying play is an immediate implication of the hegemony of the subject in the order of reality.

The self, in order to be completely identified with subjectivity, has to control the domain of its discourse so that its order remains intact. The problem with this order is at least twofold. First, the world is configured under a series of abstractions and abstract values. That is, identity is determined by a play of signifiers that are produced out of a subjectivity or productive imagination. Second, the identity of the subjective self is determined by its investments in the substitute world of signifying play. What is left out of this play is the *other* of both the world and the self. It is the loss of a pluralistic world and a variegated self.

In order to make concrete the priority of our subjectivity we had to make abstract the system that we know as the world and also inscribe our identity on its bodiless surface. The subject is the measure of all things and the subject knows itself in the production of a signifying system that ideally is universalized and closed. This is a process of totalization. It is also a repression by substitution and exclusion. This is an epistemic repression that, like and closely allied with psychological repressions, goes unnoticed until it breaks down. Then there is a return of the repressed.

The breaking of signifying systems can occur in many ways and is manifest in the formation of diverse symptoms. The frustration of not being able to make certain experiences conform to any particular signifying system threatens the adequacy of the system and will lead to a breakdown when the residue of unintelligibility becomes large enough or convolutes to overwhelm the subject. When we are not able to amend, adjust, or accommodate to changing circumstances we will try to withdraw from these circumstances. The larger the residue of anomalies, the more severe is the containment of the subject. The closure of the system is accompanied by a withering of the self. The symptom of this defense of the system is a debilitating smallness.

Some of the most sophisticated expressions of a narrowing containment are philosophical positivisms that rigidly control the domain of thinking at the expense of experience. That is, when the totalization of the subject is conjoined with a reduction of meaning, there is a shrinking of the world. This can be seen in highly self-conscious philosophical thinking or even in the retreat of a tourist to a familiar hotel room after stressful encounters with what is unfamiliar. Just as we sometimes want package tours to protect us from difference, we sometimes want package philosophy that has made all of the arrangements for meaning prior to its thinking the world. The problem with strategies of containment to ordinariness is that the world remains ordinary. The price of safety is a loss of interest and intensity. This price ironically endangers the system because in its extreme realization we loose interest in the system. Nothing matters.

Another common danger is that the conflicts between totalizing systems will relativize each other. There can be very little genuine ecumenism among totalized systems without their ceasing to be themselves. When conflict or even acquaintance between systems is forced, a familiar defense is to abstract from the specificity of the conflicting systems and claim that all is well because they are saying the same thing. The irony in this strategy is that it leads to saying nothing. These strategies are seldom conscious choices. The coinage of the Enlightenment has been so effaced that the defenses of the dominance of subjectivity seem natural. The ironic results make us ill at ease but this dis-ease is seldom properly diagnosed. We want more things, more power, more order within the domain of the subject's signifying system, but what we don't realize is that with these strategies more is less. What we feel is that meaning is lacking importance. The *real* meaning of life must be somewhere else. When this happens, the system has broken down. The inner self is felt as illusory and the sensual world is inaccessible on any other than subjective terms in a totalizing system. The Cartesian production of subjectivity with its successive amendments gradually succumbs to boredom.

There is also a very different kind of danger to totalizing systems of subjectivity that I have already referred to as the return of the repressed. This occurs when the signifying system is transgressed. We are here talking about an event and not a strategy. The incorrigibility of matter, the insistence of desire, or the pressure of external natural or historical forces tear the fabric of the system. The animality of our sexuality and death are especially common threats to the self-containment of subjective dominance. They belong to species consciousness and not private subjectivity.[2] We cannot will them out of existence even with rigorous positivistic tools. We are driven animals even unto our death.

The simple fact that we have bodies challenges the hegemony of the subject. Our bodies are our most immediate experience of the world and our most immediate experience of the incorrigibility of matter to the designs of the subject. They desire, hurt, age, and die independent of our will. It does not matter how much we condition our bodies through exercise and diet, we cannot control inevitable processes of aging or the contingencies of accidents and disease.

2. Cf. John S. Dunne, *Time and Myth* (Notre Dame: University of Notre Dame Press, 1975), pp. 60–61.

The mind/body dualism, which is a construct of mind, is also a terror to the mind that produced it. The body is a source of random violence in the domain of the subject. Not only does it often function outside of the control of consciousness, but it can intrude on the signifying play of consciousness with insistent images of morbidity or desire.

We are all familiar with those times when the body provokes a crisis of consciousness in adolescence or middle life. What is called into question at times of crisis is the importance of the ordering of the world that is in thrall to subjectivity. That is, the particular parsing of forces into the integration of the signifying play of subjective dominance fails. The subject of the self drifts outside of its identity.

It is important to note that this drift is a crisis only when the self is configured as a totalization of the subject. The possibilities for drifting can be valued very differently. A drift can be understood as a move toward the recuperation of the world that was lost in the production of subjectivity.

This, of course, does not mean that we can or want to do away with consciousness. The shift in valuation is a recognition that consciousness is something but it is not everything. What we mean by experience is consciousness and what we mean by meaning is the differential play of signifiers that constitute this consciousness. It would be absurd to talk of an unconscious knowledge or unconscious experiences, but it is not absurd to talk of unconscious forces or a conscious experience of the unconscious.[3] That which is other than consciousness, outside of the domain of subjectivity, can come into consciousness or pressure consciousness, skewing its play and distorting the figurations of its presence. Symptom formation is a liberation from the deadening abstraction of subjective dominance. The symptoms become symbols as they are both in consciousness and bespeak a reality that is other than consciousness.[4] And, in a sim-

3. Sigmund Freud, "The Unconscious," in *The Standard Edition of the Complete Psychological Works of Sigmund Freud*, translated and edited by James Strachey, 24 vols. (London: The Hogarth Press, 1957), vol. XIV, p. 160.
4. James Hillman, *Re-Visioning Psychology* (New York: Harper & Row, 1975), pp. 75–81.

ple inversion, what is symbolic is symptomatic in a system of subjective dominance.

It is not surprising that the symbol-laden religions had to be rejected, made reasonable, or made distant in the elaboration of the Enlightenment. And, for the same reasons, religion is of interest in assessing the drift of subjectivity. Its symbols are symptomatic of lines of fissure, permeable boundaries, and instabilities in consciousness. What holds an interest, even within secular thinking, are the heterogenous surfaces of the history of religions that insist themselves over against reductionistic imaginings of religion.

Religion is a pathologizing of subjective dominance. In specific traditions or communities, even the most orthodox systematizations of belief have been haunted by schisms and heterodoxies. The interest in secular studies of religion and curiosity about religion have often been channeled toward heterodox and esoteric formulations and practices because they seem to bear witness to an alterity in conscious experience.

The popular interest in the religions of others is rooted in an interest in the other of religion. What is sought is a defamiliarization of ordinary life that would fissure its repressive surfaces and give access to new intensities and forces. Since these forces are unthought, the sought-for defamiliarization is cloaked in mystery. The romantic fantasy in this interest and hope seldom comes to realization, but there can be enough of a disorientation in the encounters with religions that a return to familiar circumstances is no longer satisfying.

To find satisfaction in deeper meanings, what has to be changed is the very matrix for the production of identity. There is a need for a revaluation and thereby restructuring of the meditative beginnings of modern subjectivity. The controlling image of certainty for Descartes was what was present, clear, and distinct to consciousness. Truth was to reside in a clean, well-lighted place. It was this place that was the matrix for his meditations. There were no ruminations on the vagaries of desire. The meditations proceeded with astonishing efficiency. The world was erased and restructured in six days. Descartes did not seem to be concerned or aware that the world that he produced was a smaller world than the world that he began with.

We, like Descartes, will have to begin with the primacy of consciousness. Unlike Descartes, our method of interrogation will seek inclusion rather than exclusion. It will be messier and more experimental. It will be more a rumination than a meditation. It will be radical, but the figuration for these roots will resemble a rhizome more than a taproot of knowledge. Stems of exploration will start and stop and start again in the subsoil of experience. The tuberous root has lines of filiation that both spread and are frustrated. Truth, instead of being a clean, well-lit place, will be an experiment that will include in its data the body and its desires.[5]

The body is our most intimate experience of what is other than consciousness. We can become conscious of the body and consciousness is itself dependent upon the body. Rather than rush to a dualistic formulation, we need to note an intimate alterity in the relationship of consciousness to the body. Consciousness and the body are both more and less than each other in their relationship. They are experientially interwoven in perception and conception and the complexity of this seat of production is of direct interest to us. There is an incorrigibility of mind as well as an incorrigibility of the body, and any rethinking of the production of subjectivity and its valuation in knowledge of the world must account for both.

The peculiarity of thinking the mind is that it cannot be thought in itself. There is no purity of mind. Perception and conception are enmeshed in an otherness so that reflections of mind are always reflections of what is other than mind.

In the realm of perception, phenomenologists have referred to this characteristic presentation of mind as the intentional structure of consciousness. Consciousness takes an object. If consciousness takes itself as an object, we are then conscious of consciousness taking an

5. Gilles Deleuze and Felix Guattari, who use the rhizome as an epistemic figure, call their method of inquiry by many names including schizoanalysis, micropolitics, pragmatics, and rhizomatics. They value the fluxes, pulsions, and flows of force that did not find their way into Descartes's world. They develop a plethora of figures to explore the worlds of forces, cuts, fissures, and processes of abstraction and production (see Gilles Deleuze and Claire Parnet, *Dialogues*, translated by Hugh Tomlinson and Barbara Habberjam [New York: Columbia University Press, 1987], p. 125).

object. This notion of intentionality is not the same thing as saying that simple ideas correspond with simple sense impressions. Phenomenology is not a simple empiricism. Sense data theory is not necessarily entailed in the affirmation that we are conscious and that the perceptual manifestations of this consciousness are displays of objects. And, furthermore, this affirmation says nothing about the ontological status of conscious objects, their materiality, or their ideality.

Consciousness can only know itself in a specific heterogenous display. Intentionality implicates consciousness in a specific material and social location. It makes a difference when and where we think the experience of consciousness. It makes a difference when and where we begin the ruminations that will constitute the subjectivity of a new consciousness. What is at stake is the significance of meaning that marks the signifying play in the new subjectivity. What is at stake is the sense of what is real and important.

Three

The Incorrigibility of Mind and Transcendental Method

To cite the incorrigibility of mind is to deny any slippage into a naive realism. Consciousness may know itself in an objective display but this does not mean that the relationship to objects is immediate. Descartes's ability to put the world under erasure and reconstruct it under the aspect of subjective dominance, however problematic this construction may be, is evidence of a formative power to thinking that cannot be ignored if we are honest to our experience.

It does not seem credible that mind is a recording surface on which the world etches an impression of itself. There is evidence of a mobility, plasticity, and productivity in thinking that problematizes mirror or receptacle theories of thinking. Even the capacity for deception is an expression of a creative force in thinking. Discrepancies in perception and valuation between individuals are further evidence that within the formation of subjectivities are mediating or productive forces. How do we describe and value these forces?

What appears to us is not subjectivity but objects. Knowing that objects appear to us is not, however, the same as knowing how objects appear to us. The matrix of objective appearance is not itself thought in appearances. Until we can have access to this matrix and explore this complex of forces, we have no way to evaluate the capacity for experiencing and this includes what Schleiermacher called the capacity for religious experience. The problem is that this complex or matrix does not show itself. It is inferred from the differential play of thinking. It is particularly inferred within what in the history of Western philosophy has been called a transcendental interrogation of thinking.

Transcendental inquiry in its Kantian formulation is first of all an interrogation of the conditions of possibility for objective knowledge. The Kantian problem in the *Critique of Pure Reason* is not unlike our own.[1] The simple starting point in the first *Critique* is that all knowledge begins with experience (p. 41). But, what Kant recognizes is that this claim does not entail the further claim that all knowledge is dependent on experience. In an obvious tautological argument, he then goes on to claim that all knowledge is either dependent or not dependent on experience. There is no existential qualification of either form of knowledge. There may or may not be knowledge dependent on experience or there may or may not be knowledge independent of experience. And, we cannot simply collect expressions of knowing and ask whether they are dependent or independent of experience because we have already acknowledged that all knowledge begins with experience (pp. 41–43).

To distinguish between these two types of knowledge, Kant needed a criterion or criteria that were not simply observational. Observation would tell him that all knowledge begins with experience, although, from the very acute observations of David Hume, Kant learned that knowledge of complex ideas dependent on experience can only be probable.

What Hume noted in his interrogation of the association of simple ideas into complex ideas is that there is no simple sense impression of force, power, or necessary connection corresponding to this idea. The required linkage for complex empirical thinking was a product of an inference from our experience of two or more simple sense impressions appearing in constant conjunction with each other. Knowledge based on high degrees of probability may be an important form of knowledge, but it is not absolutely certain knowledge.[2]

1. Immanuel Kant, *Critique of Pure Reason*, translated by Norman Kemp Smith (New York: St. Martin's Press, 1965). Further page references will be cited in the text.
2. David Hume, *Enquiries Concerning the Human Understanding and Concerning the Principles of Morals* (London: Oxford University Press, 1902), pp. 60–79.

From this insight of David Hume, Kant formulated his criteria for the recognition of knowledge that was independent of experience, knowledge *a priori*. If a judgment of objective knowledge were absolutely certain, this knowledge must be knowledge independent of experience even though it is thoroughly enmeshed in experience. "Necessity and strict universality are thus sure criteria of *a priori* knowledge . . ." (p. 44). Kant was ready for the transcendental turn in his thinking. Instead of describing the world of objective appearances, he asks, "What are the conditions that make objective knowledge possible?" In the "Transcendental Aesthetic" of the first *Critique*, he claims that the formal conditions for the appearance of an object are space and time. That is, for an object to appear or be conceived, it must have spatial properties; similarly, for objects to appear or be conceived in any flux or change, they must have temporal properties. Space and time as the conditions of objective experience are necessary and of this claim we can have a certain judgment. Internal time consciousness is also a formal condition for the transcendental unity of apperception. According to these criteria, it is implied that space and time are formal properties independent of experience. They belong to the productive matrix of experience which Kant labels the transcendental imagination.[3] The specific deduction of categories in his argument are determinations of the formal necessity for space and time as conditions for the appearance and knowledge of an object. The transcendental imagination is configured as a productive force that is not only the condition for the possibilities of objective knowledge but, as such, it is a shaping force of experience and understanding.

The specific development of the Kantian schema does not seem as important to me for our inquiry in this book as the general development of the Kantian problematic. Kant determined the locus for a primary process of thinking not in the domain of appearances but in

---

3. Charles E. Winquist, *The Transcendental Imagination: An Essay in Philosophical Theology* (The Hague: Martinus Nijhoff, 1972), pp. 14–23.

a schema of productivity that is a condition of these appearances.[4] This fissuring of the productive matrix of thinking from what is thought leads to a series of separations that have continued to haunt Western thought in their incorrigibility to resolution. After the first edition of the *Critique of Pure Reason,* Kant himself tried to ameliorate the force of his insights, but even in the *Critique of Judgment* the framing of his thought is still marked by the productive force of the transcendental imagination.[5]

The gap between the objective world in-itself and the phenomenal world of appearances has never been more than metaphorically bridged. Ironically, Kant's notion of the transcendental imagination, a schema of formal determination, opens a gap of indeterminacy because it in-itself is never the object of experience.

If we are able from an interrogation of objective knowledge to establish a subjective *a priori* in the formalization of experience, we are not able, in the force of this interrogation, to conclude that the deduction of formal categories exhausts the meaning of the transcendental imagination. Kant was not describing a thing but a matrix of experience that can be likened to a complex of shaping forces. To be able to differentiate a part of this complex is, most importantly, an affirmation of such a complex. What else belongs to this complex of primary processes in conditioning the experience of the world will have to be further inferred from traces of production in the world of appearances.

If there were some obvious solution to the Kantian problem or if philosophy had been able to surpass Kant without a sleight of hand, I would not refer back to the first *Critique.* The fact that the idea of the transcendental imagination is not fashionable in post-

4. The concept of primary process thinking is usually associated with the work of Sigmund Freud, but I think that we will see that Kant's notion of a productive schema of the imagination functions in a way that is importantly similar to Freud's description of the characteristics of primary process thinking and justifies the use of this figuration in relationship to Kant's understanding.

5. Cf. Jacques Derrida, "Parergon," in *The Truth in Painting,* translated by Geoff Bennington and Ian Mcleod (Chicago: University of Chicago Press, 1987), pp. 17–147.

modern theory is a sham solution to an unresolved set of experiential problems. What is important is that the notion of a productive transcendental imagination complicated the meaning of subjectivity, thus making reason and the totalization of the subject vulnerable to a mixture of critiques that have appeared in the nineteenth and twentieth centuries. Criticism and suspicion, introduced especially by Marx, Nietzsche, and Freud, are nihilistic augmentations to the Kantian problematic only if one is committed to a construct of subjectivity that values a vision of the world exhausted in reasonableness. But, for many of us, such a rationalization of the world has belittled it, repressed desire, and emptied it of content. A loss of interest and the waning of a sense of importance in experience seem more nihilistic and a greater danger than the drift of subjectivity into ambiguities and indeterminacies. That the world may be more complicated than its Cartesian reconstruction is a relief and a hope. Depth, reality, and importance reside in the complications of experience.

There have been attempts in the history of philosophy to bring some resolution to the Kantian problematic. Many styles of neo-Kantianism developed which both idealized and romanticized the productive imagination but did so often at the expense of the concreteness of experience. For example, a dialectic directed toward the realization of a unified spirit in Hegelian idealism was rich in suggestion but led to absurd conclusions, such as the apotheosis of the Prussian state and with it an end of meaningful history.

Of course, history went on fully implicated in our animality and materiality. Idealisms wove a rich tapestry of the imagination but they did not resolve the Kantian problematic. Instead, they deepened it by showing how thinking cut loose from the incorrigibility of matter becomes only an elaboration of its capacity for endless signifying play. This is a useful demonstration that can play a part in other strategies but it did not lead to the fulfillment of the promises of idealism.

The responses to Kant that seemed to hold closest to the incorrigibilities of both mind and body were the various descriptive phenomenologies. By bracketing the question of the existential status of phenomenal appearances, phenomenology was able to be radically empirical without being reductive.[6] Phenomenology could explore the vagaries of experience and further implicate thinking into the specificities of location and period. Descriptive phenomenologies enriched and complicated the phenomenality of experience and, although they did not resolve the Kantian problem, they gave Continental philosophers a license to continue to gather experiences in a signifying play discerning and thematizing patterns of meaning within that play.

Philosophy was enfranchised with a postcritical naivete that allowed it to think experience in extreme formulations and explore phenomena that were not in clean, well-lit places. For example, Jean-Paul Sartre, a dominant figure in existentialist phenomenology, theorized a phenomenological ontology, but he also wrote and studied a literature that explored realms of darkness and absurdity.[7] Sartre and other phenomenologists troubled speculative philosophy with a range of feelings, images of sensuality, figures of desire, and the awareness of death. Existential phenomenology depended upon the power of description to be a self-authenticating hermeneutic.

A concern with meaning took precedence over a concern with reality. The criteria for evaluation were aesthetic, which may explain why so many of these philosophers allied themselves with literature or the visual arts. The danger was that philosophy would become its own justification, just as some theorists had come to understand art for art's sake. Criteria for satisfaction and authentication could become a matter of private taste and simply reinforce a culture of narcissism.

6. See the discussions of the relationships between phenomenology and American radical empiricism in John Wild's "Preface" and James M. Edie's "Introduction" to Pierre Thevenaz, *What Is Phenomenology?* (Chicago: Quadrangle Books, 1962) and in James M. Edie, "Notes on the Philosophical Anthropology of William James," in *An Invitation to Phenomenology,* edited by James M. Edie (Chicago: Quadrangle Books, 1965).

7. I think that his early theoretical work (Jean-Paul Sartre, *Being and Nothingness,* translated by Hazel Barnes [New York: Philosophical Library, 1956]) was importantly complemented by his many novels, plays, and literary studies. His later Marxist works pressure the discourse of existentialism but neither completely break from it or totally unravel it.

In spite of these dangers, the phenomenological method was a particularly rich resource for the study of religion and can be of interest for the secular as well as religious thinker in a search for significant meanings.[8] By bracketing judgments of reality and truth, phenomenologists of religion were able to gather from history, sacred texts, and the observation of practices, materials in which they could discern patterns of meaning that often had been obscured in more reductionistic and comparativist methods. They also made the study of religion responsive to what was other than Christianity in the history of world religions.

It was what was other that would often resist interpretation in familiar categories, revealing both the inadequacy of these categories and their constructedness. The phenomenology of religion has significantly contributed to the denaturalization of not only what were the prevailing understandings of religion but also to the denaturalization of the tools and products of thinking used in that understanding. The phenomenology of religion bore witness to the productive imagination and its fallibility.

Descriptive phenomenologists recognized the Kantian epistemological problem but held it in abeyance to continue their work. Transcendental phenomenologists such as Edmund Husserl did not. Martin Heidegger, very explicitly, in *Kant and the Problem of Metaphysics, What Is a Thing?*, and *Being and Time* addressed the problem of Kant's first *Critique*.[9]

In both Husserl and Heidegger, the separation between things-in-themselves and things-for-us is recognized. But, the meaning of this separation is extended. Heidegger radically reconceived the concept of the transcendental imagination in his analysis of *Dasein*. The similarity with Kant is the persistence of the transcendental project.

---

8. See Charles H. Long, *Significations: Signs, Symbols and Images in the Interpretation of Religion* (Philadelphia: Fortress Press, 1986), especially pp. 11–54.

9. Martin Heidegger, *Kant and the Problem of Metaphysics*, translated by James S. Churchill (Bloomington: Indiana University Press, 1962); *What Is a Thing?* translated by W. B. Barton, Jr., and Vera Deutsch (South Bend, IN: Gateway Editions, 1967); *Being and Time*, translated by John Macquarrie and Edward Robinson (New York: Harper & Row, 1962).

The difference is that the interrogation of the conditions of possibility for objective knowledge is shifted from an epistemological to an ontological frame. This shift was made possible by attending to the in-itself character of the knowing subject in its production of a phenomenal world. Although the world that is known is mediated by the knowing process, the knowing process is immediate to the knower, constituting a being-there in the world. The analysis of being-there [*Dasein*], which in Heidegger was closely allied to Kant's understanding of the necessity for temporal determinations, appeared to provide access to ontological understanding. The detailed working out of the analysis of temporality, *Being and Time,* gave a certain dominance to existentialist themes such as the recognition that being-there is a being toward death.

The analytic of temporality was an analytic of finitude giving rise to a discourse of anxiety, nothingness, meaninglessness, and despair. In *Being and Time* and even in the later, more poetic works of Heidegger, the Kantian problematic was reinscribed as a separation between beings and Being. Philosophy was waiting for what had called it into thinking, waiting for Godot. Transcendental and phenomenological ontology had transformed the frustration of an epistemological separation from things-in-themselves into the despair of a separation from Being.

This dark reading of Kant, describing the end of metaphysics, was dependent on the metaphysical tradition it was deconstructing. It was this tradition that had construed Being or reality as presence. It was for this tradition that it had begun the wake for the absence of Being. In theological discourse, this wake was for the death of God.

However, what is not absent is the phenomenality of experience. We are certainly tempted to turn from transcendental phenomenology back to descriptive phenomenology and assert the wager that a postcritical naivete can provide a profound engagement with the world. At least the presentation of experience would be complex and nuanced. But, the problem with this wager is that, aside from an occasional nod toward some formulation of the Kantian problematic, it is hard to distinguish its position from a precritical naive realism. Beset with the "as-if" character of its ruminations, postcritical naive thinking may be more flexible than precritical naive thinking; but it is still navigating the surfaces of the phenomenal world. It can rightly be asked whether anything has been gained by all of these convolutions of thought and whether this more sophisticated thinking has anything to say that is real and important. What we keep encountering is that thinking and talking always takes us back to the surface of phenomenal experience. We need to reframe our interrogation to acknowledge this phenomenon. The notion of a critique of pure reason has often lead to silence or an accommodation with a precritical naivete. Transcendental inquiry has to understand itself differently. Instead of a transcendental inquiry into the conditions that make objective knowledge possible, we need to be more modest and shift to a quasi-transcendental interrogation of the rules that regulate the changing surface of the phenomenal world. It is the phenomenal world that shows itself. The qualification of quasi-transcendental is the recognition that we are not unveiling ontological structures that regulate being-there in the world but rules that in any specific situation regulate the differential play of appearances.

First, it should be noted that there is a difference and a relationship between perception and conception on the phenomenal surface of experience. The important similarity is that they are both differential in their manifestations. We perceive in contrasting figurations. We do not see a black cow against the horizon of a black night. Sensory images are only known in contrast. The more vivid the contrast the more intense is our phenomenal perception if the contrasting elements stay within the threshold of sensory perception.

This sensate world of perception is an imaginal domain. We experience images and not trees, boats, or dogs. In this imaginal domain, the images are not bound to their originary experiences. Once I have seen a dog, I can imagine the dog, dream the dog, and skew the image of the dog in the theater of memory.

I can also name the dog. The naming of the animals may be fundamentally indistinguishable from the Adamic sin of eating of the tree of knowledge. The transition from percept to concept, the transition from image to sign, is first of all a naming and the name that is attached to an image can also be substituted for the image. The name is a sign and we pass from an imaginal domain to a semiotic domain and sometimes mix the two. The strange feature in naming is that there need not be any similarity between the name and the image to which it is attached or for which it is substituted.

There are two domains of difference in consciousness. We are conscious in the imaginal domain but we are not yet thinking. At least there appears to be an experiential distinction between an imaginal display, the presentment of images, and the processes of a differential play of signs, semiosis. Signifying, the play of signs, is a combinatory movement of signs that places them in relationship to each other, thereby inscribing them on various recording surfaces and shifting their combinations.

Speech and writing are paradigmatic of semiotic processes but semiosis is not limited to speech and writing. In the visual arts the images of an imaginal display become signs that then can be reproduced in differing combinations. The images become signs for images just as words can become signs for images. To think the world is first of all to substitute signs for images, even when the signs are first experienced as the presentment of images. This thinking, semiosis, is, as named by Freud, a secondary process. The primary process, which is inferred in the secondary process from the necessity for differentiation in consciousness, is in the complex of forces we have, following Kant, been calling the transcendental imagination.

Semiosis is a continual augmentation of consciousness through new configurations of differential contrast. These can be configurations of sound, colors, words, or mixtures of signs as in a Magritte painting. Regularities in consciousness appear in relationship to the repetition of combinatory forms regulating the configurations of differential contrast.

Syntax in language is the normalization of combinatory forms through repeated usage and conventional agreement. In more exact semiotic systems such as mathematics or logic, a project within the systems has been to bring the combinatory forms to explicit awareness and articulation. The failures of these projects have ironically led to important insights into the incompleteness of semiotic systems and the inability to fully rationalize secondary process thinking even if we make the shift to quasi-transcendental analysis. The rules for the formation of discourse are always implicated in that which is other than the semiotic systems that they regulate. A fissure marking the complex of forces in primary process thinking keeps opening the secondary process of thinking, but what is available to be thought is always the surface display of differences.

Why does this recurring problem interest us when we have already noted the richness of understanding that can come with wagering for the naivete of descriptive phenomenologies? Or, we could simply step back from the Kantian problematic and elaborate a signifying play of signs until it satisfies us like reading a good novel. This would be more of a diversion from than a solution to the problem.

However, besides being tried and tired, these moves, which would hold us to the surface of signifying play, are no longer innocent. The incompleteness and indeterminacy of the product of signifying play has introduced possibilities of distortion and deception in our experience of the world and in the inscription of our own identity within it. We cannot ignore the possibility that the loss of intensity and diminished sense of importance within experience may be related to the semiotic process and not just its product. Our sense of reality and importance depend on this process and, unless we can come to some consciousness of its functions and of the forces that are involved in its functioning, we are uncritical victims of an identity that is inscribed for us on the phenomenal surface of its differential play. If identity is in difference, to have an identity is to be implicated in an otherness of signs. That which is other in the configuration of differential contrasts that constitute our identity is internally related to us and thus, although a matter of difference, it is not a matter of indifference.

What is at stake is how we are written into the text of our world. Not only are we written into the world but the world is written in the semiotic process. This writing and rewriting of the world is what I keep referring to as the incorrigibility of mind. We have knowledge of neither a world nor a self that is not textualized in differential contrasts. The process and the elements within the process—images, signs, the representation of images as signs, syntactical conventions—are what make the difference, what make the phenomenal world. The forces that shape a language also shape a world. This has relevance in both primary and secondary processes of semiotic production. Much of the importance of Marx, Nietzsche, and Freud in our inquiry is how they came to insights that are importantly similar to this claim and brought them to articulation in the specificity of their interrogations. They deepened and complicated the Kantian problem by introducing into its basic matrix forces of distortion, disguise, and deceit.

Marx and Freud developed their hermeneutics of suspicion by thinking the importance of the pathological symptoms on the surfaces of our social and personal lives. Nietzsche, with a poetic violence, pathologized the conventions of discourse, revealing the general metaphoricity and constructedness of all language uses. Truth, in Nietzsche's judgment, was a "mobile army of metaphors, metonyms and anthropomorphisms."[10] In combination, these three thinkers inflicted a severe wound to the phenomenological solution of the Kantian problem and cast doubt on the integrity of any of the descriptive human sciences.

As already noted, descriptive phenomenologies acknowledged the separation between the phenomenal and noumenal worlds, bracketed the question of noumenal truth, and sought for meaning in the phenomenal display of experience. What was not fully appreciated was that in the matrix of forces regulating the appearance of phenomena, there might be not only forces that regulate the formal qualities of experience, but, also, more cunning forces of displacement, distortion, and deceit leaving their mark on the manifestations of appearances.

10. Friedrich Nietzsche, "On Truth and Lie in an Extra-Moral Sense," in *The Portable Nietzsche*, edited and translated by Walter Kaufmann (New York: Penguin Books, 1976), p. 46.

Prior to any interpretive work within the secondary processes of thinking, it is possible that the appearance of the world is already subject to interpretations in the interests of desire, social class, or the will to power. It is the indeterminant knowledge of the transcendental imagination, the schema for determination, that opens the door for the serious philosophical reception of ideas from Marx, Nietzsche, and Freud. If experiences are distorted in the primary processes of presentation, descriptive strategies will repeat these distortions in their representations.

For all three of these thinkers, it is the nonidentity between human subjectivity and what I have been calling the transcendental imagination that provides the possibility for exchanging a heterological infrastructure to consciousness for the Kantian transcendental unity of apperception. The Marxist hidden laws of social formation, Freud's unconscious drives, and Nietzsche's power that wills the pulsions and fluxes of forces decenter the matrix of consciousness so that the formation of a unified concept of subjectivity is a false consciousness. Even the claim that we experience a unity of apperception is a secondary construction forced on the phenomenality of experience.

Freud's discovery of the unconscious is first of all an accounting for discontinuities in experience. Dreams, slips of the tongue, neuroses and psychoses all bear witness in the idiom of psychological understanding to heterology rather than unity in the ordering of experience. Although consciousness is identified with the secondary process, it is not independent from the primary heterological processes. Over the scope of Freud's work, this insight has implications not only for personal psychology but for the interpretation of culture.

His analysis of dream work, the transformation of a latent dream thought into manifest dream content, is a model for the full analysis of culture in which infrastructural forces of experience are manifested as a world content.[11] The dream work, in a divided loyalty to the satisfaction of drives and the protection of fragile constructions of

11. See Paul Ricoeur, *Freud and Philosophy: An Essay on Interpretation*, translated by Denis Savage (New Haven: Yale University Press, 1970), pp. 159–77.

subjectivity, is a work of displacement, substitution, representation, and secondary revision. Not only do the drives manifest themselves in disguise, but, since the domain of their appearance is always itself a differential field of referential order, all of the elements in that field are implicated in the distortion of the disguise. The libidinal economy of bodily desires is woven through the fabric of appearances.

The productive forces of primary process thinking make culture a psychological ideology in which desire can be squandered as well as satisfied. When the formation and secondary elaboration of subjectivity are not adequate for the expression and satisfaction of desire, life goes on but it loses its intensity.

Very similar comments can be made about Marx and the decentering and revising of the concept of the transcendental imagination. For Marx, the matrix of productivity is materialistic. The hidden laws of social formation condition the appearance of the world so that once again a centered notion of the human subject is displaced. The very appearing of the world, not only its secondary elaborations and valuations, is implicated in politics, class interests, and other social pressures. As with Freud, the phenomenality of the world is an ideological display; with Marx, the body of drives and interests is a social body.

We don't have to make a choice between Freud and Marx on this level of interrogation. They combine to bring to the aesthetic formulation of the transcendental imagination a complex nexus of physical, material, and social forces. The transcendental imagination can no longer be simply identified with subjectivity, although subjectivity conditioned by specific material drives, libidinal and social forces is its product. To have any measure of the self, transcendental inquiry will need to be complemented by ideology critique.

A linkage between the contributions of Freud and Marx can be further elaborated if we include in our analysis the radical troping of truth by Nietzsche. Nietzsche dislodged truth from any absolute grounding by attacking the patriarchal hierarchy of Western metaphysics through enigmatic aphorisms and through a direct appropriation of Kant. But he also accuses Kant of retreat from the liberating insights of the first *Critique* when he could not accept the dizzying implications of his own theory of the transcendental imagination.[12]

It is a loss of a grip on truth in the realm of pure reason which made the discovery of a categorical imperative in the realm of practical reason and ethics so important to Kant. But, from Nietzsche's perspectivalism, this categorical imperative is itself a construction that is as empty as it is universal. It marks no gain over the loss of confidence in the truth of pure reason.

Truths are fictions imaginatively produced in a play of differences with specific genealogies. Truth is not found. It is a way of looking that masks the fluxes and flows of the will to power. The troping of truth in Nietzsche is a turn to the arbitrariness of the elements of language. He liberates the productive imagination in a celebration of the endless possibilities for world-making and for surpassing the rigidified experience of the human condition. He calls us not to a realm of transcendence but to the transcendence of the self. It is a call to live dangerously. Anything else would be "bovine mediocrity."

The more sober legacy of this pyrotechnic thinking is the recognition of the general metaphoricity of all language uses and the arbitrariness of truth. "At best, existence is revealed as a palimpsest of fictions which the human imagination invents for itself in order to experience an endless multiplicity of meanings."[13] As any reader of Nietzsche knows, this experience is not nothing. The loosening of language usage in perspectival metaphoricity is also a dance with the intensities of fluxes and flows of force. It is a living dangerously

---

12. "And now don't cite the categorical imperative, my friend! . . . It makes me think of the old Kant who had obtained the 'thing in itself' by *stealth*—another very ridiculous thing!—and was punished for this when the 'categorical imperative' crept stealthily into his heart and led him *astray—back* to 'God,' 'soul,' 'freedom,' and 'immortality,' like a fox who loses his way and goes astray back into his cage" (Friedrich Nietzsche, *The Gay Science,* translated by Walter Kaufmann [New York: Vintage Books, 1974], p. 264).

13. Richard Kearney, *The Wake of Imagination* (Minneapolis: University of Minnesota Press, 1988), p. 214.

because the forces are not stabilized in a unity of meaning. We begin to see that the figure of the will to power might better be inverted to say that power wills in the production of a multiplicity of meanings. The signs are arbitrary markings and metaphors are combinatory effects of the fluxes of power.

All of the metaphorical truths are arbitrary. Only a letting-go is a truth that is not arbitrary. In the world of the complete arbitrariness of signs, this truth of letting-go is the willing of the eternal recurrence of the same.

This Nietzschean response to the arbitrariness of the realm of signs is a strategic deracination of ordinariness. In both philosophy and ordinary life the more usual response is the development of metaphorical strategies. Seldom are these highly conscious strategies because the sense of the arbitrariness of signs, outside of philosophy and linguistics, is usually vague and interwoven with fantasies of a romantic imagination and the genius of creativity.

A metaphorical strategy capitalizes on the general metaphoricity of discourse without acknowledging this investment. That is, the conjunctive power of the word *is* allows for a rapid expansion of conscious experience without the attendant awareness that this consciousness is based on configurations of contrast that have themselves no necessity or ontological weight. They satisfy us by texturizing the textuality of discourse and in this way compensate for the frightening sense of contingency in life.

We are willing to give the widest latitude for the production of metaphors in those discourses that are imbued with a sense of importance and that also resist stabilization in conventional patterns of speech because of their experiential vagueness. Life's passages that consciously implicate us in forces that are other than ourselves are particularly given over to uncritical metaphorical expansion. The metaphorical strategy values the metaphor as a metaphor even if it doesn't recognize it as such.

However, the metaphorical strategy is hard to sustain. Through common usage the metaphor is effaced as metaphor. If the signs in the metaphorical construction are images used as signs and the metaphor is effaced, the images become reality. The vitality of the metaphor is lost when it masquerades as reality. In our contemporary culture it can be noted that sometimes the effacement of metaphor as metaphor is intended. That is, there can be a double strategy of construction and effacement. Then the illusion of reality can be a tool of manipulation. This double strategy can be referred to as a commodification of the image. The metaphorical construction through likeness of dissimilars gives a credibility to the appearance that when its metaphoricity is effaced leaves the image not in a state of *likeness* but in a state of *isness*. The image is now the reality and it is the image that is valued.

This transformation of images into reality permeates contemporary life from the selling of material products to the selling of information. The power of the image as reality is the power of its metaphorical constitution, which has been effaced. The image cannot deliver the promise of giving access to reality.

The reason that a metaphor has power and not just meaning in a signifying play is that there is always a differential gap in the bringing together of what is dissimilar in the formation of the metaphor. The interstices in the framework of metaphorical construction allow for the fluxes and pulsions of force to flow through the discourse and are in this sense pressuring the discourse without ever becoming the object or content of the discourse. The effacement of metaphoricity closes this gap and sterilizes the discourse, making it only a play of meaning. Here meaning loses power. Experience is dulled. Consistency and safety are purchased at the price of intensity. The world is filled with meanings that have no importance. The image as commodity is a reality that is a parody of reality.

Four

The Incorrigibility of the Body and the Refiguring of Discourse

When Descartes sat in front of his fire for a third night of meditation, he sought to recover the world that was other than subjectivity. Interestingly, his assertion of subjective dominance in the *cogito* of the second mediation meant that he had to work within the confines of its domain.

He was able, within this constraint, to assert three possible sources for ideas. He writes: "Among these ideas, some seem to be born with me, others to [be alien to me and to] come from without, and the rest to be made [and invented] by myself."[1] The problem that immediately confronts Descartes and his reader is that one can't simply ask from which source particular ideas come. To make that determination, since all ideas are manifested in the domain of subjectivity, the ideas need to reveal traces of their origination. For Descartes, the criteria for making this judgment were completely within the domain of subjectivity, even when one is talking about the concept of ideas with sources outside of subjectivity. It is subjectivity that makes this judgment.

In what retrospectively appears to be a peculiarly postmodern argument, Descartes convolutes subjectivity in its own productivity by exploring the limits of its powers. In seeking for what is outside of subjectivity he doesn't turn toward empirical objects because in the first day of meditation he had already disqualified unequivocal access

---

1. René Descartes, *Discourse on Method and Meditations,* translated by Laurence J. LaFleur (Indianapolis and New York: The Liberal Arts Press, 1960), p. 94. Further page references will be cited in the text.

to the objective world through his method of radical doubt. To reach out to an objective world he needed a foundation from within subjectivity that to him seemed clearly and distinctly certain. It is from a subjective foundation that he recovers an objective world. His move is surprising. It is the *idea* of "God" that he interrogates at the extremities of subjectivity. The force of his argument is that he cannot convince himself that the idea of God could either be innate or invented and therefore it must come from outside. His concept of God is of an infinite substance, eternal, immutable, independent, omniscient, omnipotent, and the creator of all things (p. 101). Descartes claimed that the more attentively I considered the attributes of this concept of God, "the less I can persuade myself that I could have derived them from my own nature" (p. 101).

It would seem to a reader in the twentieth century that this argument is less a proof for the existence of God than the use of the concept of God to trope the discourse of subjectivity and transgress its domain. The "Third Meditation" is a demonstration that subjectivity cannot contain itself and thereby can witness to what is other than its discourse. God is a figuration within subjective discourse that disrupts hegemony of the subject over all experience. God means what discourse is not.[2] The conceiving of God is an argument against idealistic solipsism. It enfranchises consideration of that which is other than subjectivity from within subjectivity. This sense of the other is a theological exigency of mind. Talk of God is incorrigible to the assertion of subjective dominance.

Still, this theological crack in subjectivity does not give any immediate access to an objective world. Consciousness is still phenomenal consciousness. What is different is that understanding can at least experiment with the possibility that the heterogeneity of the phenomenality of experience may be implicated in that which is other than subjectivity. It is the impurities in discursive practices that are most interesting for this thinking and might be thought of as secular theological traces within the discourse. We need to ask: "What is

---

2. See Robert P. Scharlemann, "The Being of God When God Is Not Being God," in *Deconstruction and Theology* (New York: Crossroad, 1982), pp. 79–108.

incorrigible within the differential play of thinking?" God-talk is not easily accessible and the attributes Descartes ascribes to God are not obvious in a secular milieu. In a contemporary context, to rethink the "Third Meditation," the figurations of otherness that trope the discourse and disrupt the hegemony of the subject are not going to be traditional theological formulations, even though they may function like Descartes's God.

For example, Jean-Paul Sartre, in discussing the *cogito* of Descartes, refers to the incorrigible givens within experience, a contingent situatedness, as facticity.[3] It is facticity that limits freedom and constrains consciousness. It is the pressure from what is other than subjectivity, although it will be known only under the conditions of consciousness. For Freud, facticity would be the reality principle. We can dream quixotic dreams and imagine utopias, but we discover in the specificity and particularity of experience a certain regularity of appearances that are not malleable to our discursive practices. There are certain appearances that persist and resist shaping.

In surveying the range of human experiencing still within the range of subjectivity, I want to refer to the first figure of facticity as the incorrigibility of the body because our most intimate experience of facticity is the persistence of our animality and its resistance to change and substitute satisfactions. Bodily drives press for recognition and satisfaction. Even when disguised in displacements, repressions, and substitutions, not only is subjectivity symptomatically marked, there are also regular experiences of the return of the repressed undermining the order of things. All of this can be witnessed on the phenomenal surfaces of experience.

Experiences that resist shaping and persist in pressuring the differential play of consciousness mark the incorrigibility of the other of the body and the economy of forces in which it is situated. These constellations of power are often in tension with the configurations

3. Jean-Paul Sartre, *Being and Nothingness: An Essay on Phenomenological Ontology,* translated by Hazel Barnes (New York: Philosophical Library, 1956), pp. 79–84.

of discourse. Because talk comes up short in ordering these experiences, they are analogous to Descartes's talk of God in the "Third Meditation." We have trouble convincing ourselves that images and ideas at play in these experiences are either innate within or invented by our subjectivity. Facticity is a mark of the adventitious.

Although the "other" of consciousness challenges the order formed in the construction of subjectivity and thereby threatens the stability of the self, we are fascinated and drawn toward these experiences because of their intensity. It is here that consciousness surpasses its own discourse. We might say that the markings of the incorrigibility of the other are an elementary transcendence of the subject.

The phenomenality of this elementary transcendence is complicated. First, the sense of the other of our animality is not private. Our hunger, sexuality, and sensuality implicate the other of the body with the bodies of others. Desire of the other is also the desire to be desired by the other. Subjectivity is given over to a complexity of relationships to objects and other subjects. Second, this complexity is always specifically located. It has a place. It is, however, not a simple place. The sense of place is complicated through many figurations.

For example, the land, sea, sky, and city are traditional expressions of place that seem beyond the control of mind. To this list we can add the forces of history, economy, and even language as further specifications of location.

In everyday experience it is not uncommon to seek a sense of the land or sea or city as definitions of ourselves. Whether it be the big sky country of Montana or the rocky shores of a Greek island, we seek the experience of the other of place as a confrontation with the other of self. Part of the appeal of travel is that in it we find satisfaction in an odd rhythm of defamiliarization and appropriation. We try to vacate the ordinary order of things as we go to the sea or confront the brute facticity of mountains.

These confrontations with place, including a sense of a place in history, strain the capacity for thinking identity in the ordinary differential play of language. Semiosis, the play of signs, elaborates itself in a poiesis to better reach toward the other of subjectivity. This, however, is not a straightforward move. We cannot simply escape the mind and the machinations of thinking through discourse in an appeal to the other.

Poiesis is itself a semiotic process. No matter how rich the texturing of language, talk is talk. Poiesis is a reconfiguration within discourse and not an escape from it. We might think of poiesis as a refiguring of discourse to make space for the incorrigibility of the other within discourse. There can be poetic elaborations of the land or sea just as a visual artist can elaborate landscapes or seascapes.

This poetic elaboration is an insistence on meeting. Metaphoric constructions bring about the meeting of dissimilars, intensify contrasts, and space the places of resistance. It is the conjunction of the images or ideas of subjectivity with the incorrigibles of materiality that give us something to hold on to when the images or ideas fail to be realized. We can depend on the regularity of the sun's rising or the endurance of stones in their mute transcendence of discourse.

The incorrigibility of bodily libido also can be elaborated narratively into a story. We have romantic stories, tragic stories, and psychoanalytic stories that variously plot the itinerary of libidinal forces as they course through our lives. These stories are not descriptions of the other of thinking as much as constructions that can be inhabited by these forces of alterity. The mark of habitation is intensity. We fall in love when the libidinal forces are integrated into a story that includes our sense of self. This is much more intense than when we tell a story that does not provide spaces for the disruption and presence of bodily, material, or historical forces.

It is not enough that we can tell a good story, write history, or poetically elaborate material figurations of place. There must be a spacing within these constructions for resistances, flows, and pressures of the other of discourse. These spacings are not subject matter. There are many visual or literary landscapes or seascapes that mask the incorrigibility of place. Pornography is often a repression of libidinal forces in the objectification and sterilization of the human body.

What is needed is a refiguring of discourse in a mixed genre of force and meaning. This refiguring is a variation and radicalization of the metaphoric strategy. The poetic and narrative elaboration of figures of discourse is a texturing within textuality to give space for place, space for body, space for libido, and space for history. These elaborations, which can be theological, are a preparatory cultivation of the text for the investment of libidinal and material forces. The text will neither describe nor contain these forces in themselves. They are other than text. Texts are simulacra. But, as a domain of appearances, texts are perspectives within the complex of forces that constitute place. Texts are places of meeting, theaters of conjunction and confrontation between the incorrigibilities of mind and body. The forces themselves do not appear on the stage. They appear and disappear like the lighting and shadows that surround and infiltrate the play of the text. They condition the appearance of the text and at the same time are conditioned by the text. They mark the text; but, the text is also a cutting, coupling, and marking of the forces. The theater of intersections, a theater of cruelty, is a dialectic of act and content, force and meaning.

The problem in accessing force is that the dialectic is masked by the totalization and closure of the signifying play of the semiotic production. There must be a turn, a trope, in the discourse of presentation to break the dominance of appearances. When the lights go off on the stage we immediately become aware of our animality, our place in theater. We grip the armrests of our seats or touch the person sitting next to us. We feel a rush of anxiety in the brokenness of the presentation. We experience a shock and "discourse loses its momentum."[4]

The radicalization of the metaphoric strategy is a transgression of semiotic closure. This play requires a place. It has a context, a location in a nexus of forces. The scene of origination, the scene of production, is only known in a scene of transgression. Transgression is a realization of the dialectic between content and context. The context is active, pulsating, and flowing. It is always becoming. The content

4. George Santayana, in a sustained argument against idealistic solipsism, has a profound understanding of discourse as an experience that is subject to the shock of our animality. The figure of the lights going out on the stage is one of his illustrations in *Scepticism and Animal Faith* (New York: Dover Publications, 1955), p. 139.

is a cut, a slice, and an instantiation within the contextual process. The play of differences is a contextual process that includes the cuts, dislocations, and substitutions of discourse. Identities in difference are the flickering moments of contrast that are marked on a recording surface of speech, writing, painting, photography, or other semiotic systems. Identity is always in the making.

The strategy of generating a mixed discourse is a representation of the dialectic between act and content achieved by actively folding discourse on itself. This folding is an experiment in writing that is also an experiment in reading. The differential play of thinking is first of all an occasion and place for the habitation of forces. More accurately, thinking locates itself in a nexus of forces and it is this specification of location that implicates force in discourse. Habitation is the specific semiotic scaffolding of discursive practices.

Second, within the differential play of thinking, discourse can fold itself, convolute its surface, revealing the fissures of what we might call the interstices of metaphoric figuration. The tropes are troped so that they are a content as well as a structuration of the discourse. They reveal themselves as stressed, fissured, and incomplete. The discourse is loosened throughout. Inclusion and expansion give way to deconstructive drift. And, it is this drift and not a new content that is the desideratum of the experiment. It is the drift that transgresses the totalization and repressiveness of discursive practices. It is the drift that is an ethical and political resistance to totalitarian thinking.

Deconstructive drift is an effect of a work of thinking and its achievement does not imply a prescription of any particular rules for the formation of discourse, writing, or reading. The work is a sustained critique of literalism that is applicable to any textual formations.

For example, the postmodern declarations of the end of history, the end of the novel, or the closure of the book cannot be universalized. These claims are localized and situational. If the novel as a genre of literature came to an end with Joyce's *Finnegan's Wake,* it came to an end for its modernist European and North American readers. Strangely, these same readers continue to read Gabriel García Marquez along with a whole new generation of second- and third-world novelists as well as the Joyce of the *Portrait* and *Ulysses*. For those readers not in the avant-garde of modernism, nothing happened with the publication of *Finnegan's Wake*. Popular culture has been little disturbed by the momentous closures announced in the pages of learned journals.

I do not mean to suggest that popular culture is the measure of importance for a culture or that the exhaustion of an art form is unimportant. What I do want to suggest is that the recognizable credibility of any discursive formation is specific to situation and particular reading practices. Experiments in writing that torture the text and transgress its literality have been especially helpful in forcing criticism toward a more complex awareness of the semiotic process, but they need not be paradigmatic or prescriptive for the future of writing. Most important, they have taught us to read nonliterally. They have taught us how to fold the text even when the text does not convolute naturally.

For example, philosophers such as Derrida and Deleuze have used experiments in philosophic writing to open up experiments in philosophic reading. Plato, Spinoza, Kant, and Nietzsche are read against the grain of closure within fluxes and complexes of forces giving their work an intensity that more literal reading strategies repress. The deconstruction of philosophy has been an insistence on the importance of philosophy and an affirmation of the possibilities for a continual reading of philosophy.

This does not mean that if we learn how to read deconstructively that all texts are of equal value and worth reading. Some texts are richer in their complexity and comprehensiveness than others. Some texts are more congenial to analysis and interrogation than others. In some texts we more easily recognize our interests than in others.

The recognition of interest is not always explicitly conscious. More commonly there is a resonance with a text or elements within a text that when brought into patterns of intertextual referencing can become conscious. We can be drawn into a text or be chosen by a text because it can work upon us, thus implicating our interests.

What this means is that the texts that are current in our thinking and through which we inscribe our identity can be implicated through intertextual referencing with new texts. Not only are new texts complexified by abutting old texts, but, if the metaphoric range of the new texts is greater than the range of the old texts, the complexification is understood in figures of depth and importance.

Therefore the space of textual habitation can be both transformed and enlarged. Intertextual referencing and the resultant metaphoric complexification are preparations of the surface of the text for deconstructive drift. This preparatory work implicates a wider range of experiences in the drift and is in this way transformative of experience. That is, a wider range of experience is implicated in that which is other than subjectivity through a work within the subjective domain. As previously noted, a habitation, a lattice work of construction, precedes deconstruction.

This is a move that Descartes made in his "Third Meditation"; but, as we have already suggested, his particular move is a move that is very difficult in a secular milieu because secular thinkers do not share with Descartes the incredulity that the idea of God could be factitious. The traditions of Feuerbach, Marx, and Freud give a very modern credibility to the idea that the idea of God is both factitious and a projection of human needs. A new construction, a new theology, will be a necessary preparation for transgressing the domain of subjectivity. If Descartes's move is still possible, it is only possible if the idea of God can be recuperated at the extremities of conscious experience.

Appeals to the world's great mythological and religious traditions as routes carrying experience to its extremities are not faulted by the failures of these traditions to be comprehensive and internally complex. The problem in a secular milieu is the lack of self-recognition in these traditions. The diverse hermeneutics of suspicion have shadowed the hermeneutics of recognition in the articulation of identities.

As yet, the work of the critical theorist has not been able to adequately access and assess the work of the historian of religions and mythographer. The articulation and elaboration of identities in stone, sacrament, and ritual, the transformation of events in narrative or epic, and theological understandings of word as event and inter-rogator of the listener are secondary subtexts to the dominant ide-ologies of secular consciousness.

Neither secular nor religious texts can be exclusively thought on their own terms if these great traditions were to be vitally accessible to contemporary life. The question is how to think secular con-sciousness on other than its own terms. The problem is not dissimi-lar from problems that surface in attempts at interreligious dialogues among the world's religions. As Paul Tillich suggested in *Christian-ity and the Encounter of the World Religions,* to enter into deep con-versations with the world's religions a Christian will have to speak out of the depths of Christian experience.[5] It is difficult to understand another tradition on a deeper level than you can understand your own or yourself. This means that a real encounter with the religious traditions would first require a refiguring of secular discourse for complexity, depth, or "bigness." This work may not be temporally prior to deconstruction, but it is presupposed by a theological decon-structive hermeneutic.

The refiguring of secular discourse is first of all a complexifica-tion of discourse by a letting-go of reductive strategies. The "letting-go" is a positive act of valuation. It is a saving of appearances, the nonreduction of the phenomenality of experience.

It requires a strength to live in the ambiguity and heterogeneity of appearances, and the danger is that we will skew the hovering attention of the letting-go toward the dismissal of those experiences that resist organization. Consciousness has to ruminate among the flickerings of its own productions even to the point that it becomes a problem to itself. Secular discourse has to risk wandering out of mind if it is to let go of reductionistic strategies.[6]

Second, the refiguration of secular discourse is allowing thought

5. Paul Tillich, *Christianity and the Encounter of the World Religions* (New York: Columbia University Press, 1963), p. 97.

6. James Hillman in a psychological idiom has referred to what I am calling "let-ting go" as "pathologizing" or "falling apart." "As such, pathologizing is a hermeneu-tic which leads events into meaning" (*Re-Visioning Psychology* [New York: Harper & Row, 1975], p. 111).

the freedom that follows the catharsis of radical criticism. If secular discourse is to plumb its depth or measure its complexity, it cannot be enthralled to the minimalist expressions that often follow the cathartic achievement of criticism. For example, the denials of narrative literalism, master narratives or the totalization of discourse are not a denial of narrative construction. Arguments against being able to think the transcendental signified are epistemological and not metaphysical arguments. These arguments cannot make claims beyond the domain of textual differentiation without contradicting themselves. It is precisely for this reason that textuality can be refigured and complexified in the strength of radical criticism. Textuality can be minimally abstract or richly textured and ornamented.

Postmodern textuality can be like postmodern architecture—borrowing and representing from any of the traditions that precede it. Criticism cannot delimit the possibilities for bricolage. The letting-go is the opening for theological work. It is an opening to the pressures at hand, the incorrigibilities of body and mind.

What I have been describing is not a simple procedure of steps that follow one another. The various moves interpenetrate each other. These are processes of becoming. Openings and closures repeat and follow each other. Complicating and deepening secular consciousness in theological discourse is a permanent critique and, in some sense, a permanent revolution.[7]

---

7. Cf. Jean-François Lyotard, *Driftworks* (New York: Semiotext(e), 1984), p. 32.

Five

Theological Text Production

Just as Eve came from Adam's rib, just as Venus was born out of the waves, Agnes sprang from the gesture of that sixty-year-old woman at the pool who waved at the lifeguard and whose features are already fading from my memory. At the time, that gesture aroused in me immense, inexplicable nostalgia, and this nostalgia gave birth to the woman I call Agnes.

Milan Kundera, *Immortality*

The gesture that Kundera refers to in his novel may be thought of as a singularity that issues forth in a series of significations that gives birth to a new identity, the woman he calls Agnes.[1] The gesture is specific and even though it can be repeated, the specificities of its time and place make it unique, make it a singularity. That is, the gesture can be repeated but the gesture as an event is singular. Agnes is not a universal identity, and the working out of her character in the novel is the further specification of a stream of meaning that also is neither abstract nor universal.

Although it might appear that Agnes is a product of Kundera's imagination and within the domain of his subjectivity, there would be no Agnes without the gesture at the swimming pool. Furthermore, Agnes commences to leave a Cartesian frame of subjectivity as soon as she is born. Agnes is an emission from a single gesture of a series of significations that must come to expression for her to be understood and have an identity. The gesture was like a particular throw of the dice, repeatable but never the same and always subject to chance. We never know in advance what a particular throw of the dice will mean.

1. The notion of a singularity is developed by Gilles Deleuze in *The Logic of Sense* (translated by Mark Lester [New York: Columbia University Press, 1990]) and it will be basic element in the development of this chapter. Hereafter cited in the text as LS with the appropriate page numbers.

Kundera has a profound sense of the singularities that populate his novels. They are expressed in various languages of chance, contingency, gesture and metaphor. Whether it be Agnes's gesture at the swimming pool or Pharaoh's daughter picking a bulrush basket out of the Nile, the meaning of events escape the frame of the Cartesian self as universal subjectivity. Part of what we mean by meaning is specificity. It is in his commitment to the meaning of events that might have gone unnoticed that Kundera is an easy ally to enlist in the development of understanding a heterological infrastructure for subjectivity. In the thickness of description in his novels there are no characters that would not lose their identities through assimilation to a universal subjectivity. If Kundera had not noticed that specific gesture by the swimming pool, we would not know Agnes. It is possible that there are many lives, a gift of meaning, that slip by us because we don't know how to see and we don't know how to think.

Kundera knows that he is writing in an "enlightened" world where "reason" is privileged. He also knows that "reason" is an ambivalent notion and not always adequate to the development of a novel or the fictive achievements of life. In *Immortality* he ponders the meaning of "reason." "First, it designates the ability to think, and only second, the cause. Therefore reason in the sense of a cause is always understood as something rational. . . . But in German, a reason in the sense of a cause is called *Grund,* a word having nothing to do with the Latin *ratio* and originally meaning 'soil' and later 'basis.' . . . I am trying to grasp the *Grund* hidden at the bottom of each of my characters, and I am convinced more and more that it has the nature of a metaphor."[2]

Grund is a metaphor for metaphor. Kundera is far outside of the ontotheological tradition in which the search for a ground is the search for a metaphysical first principle. A metaphor may be the singularity of an event but it is embedded in soil. It has place in a nexus of material and physical forces, including the body, and from it there is an emission of meaning that involves a differential play among forces, images, and signifiers. Meaning is not reducible to any of its

2. Milan Kundera, *Immortality* (New York: Grove Weidenfeld, 1991), p. 237.

constitutive elements. That is why description must always be thick. A theology that is only referential to the arbitrations of a constructed pure subjectivity has lost its ground. It has difficulty elaborating itself in a thickness of meaning. A theology of subjective presence is simply too thin. All of the hidden forces are anomalies in the range of its gaze. It cannot understand or speak to Agnes or any other of the lives that populate our world. It is not surprising that theology with its complicated and overdetermined voices has come to mean a loss of meaning and significance in a secular milieu. First, the adoption of the Cartesian subject as a referential ground for meaning was an abstraction from the ground that is the metaphorical soil of life; and, second, the catharsis of radical criticism deracinating the Cartesian identity of being and thinking left all meaning floating in an endless play. It is simply not enough to say no to Descartes and the Enlightenment. A new thinking about thinking is required before we can rethink the meaning of theological thinking.

We have already begun this process with the radical catharsis of deconstructive criticism. Deconstruction has cleared a space for experimental constructions, although it will be an unstable space because it must include within its domain the pressure of its own deconstructive achievement.

Experimental constructions are tentative and heuristic. They anticipate an intelligibility but it is an intelligibility that will only be known in its expression. In some ways the constructive move is always a preparation for deconstructive drift and, because it is postcritical, the construction is already implicated in the moves that are to follow.

A postdeconstructive, postcritical construction is not going to be rooted in new ground. Kundera's *Grund* is a metaphor. We are always going to be talking about metaphors and other tropes within discursive practices. We could start a discussion of construction with roots and grounds as long as we realize that they are metaphors, but I think a more neutral figure for talking about the beginning of heuristic constructions is the frame. The frame is less organic, clearly constructed, more contingent, and temporary. Whether or not discourse can be grounded, it is always framed. The metaphoricity of roots and grounds is itself framed in any particular discursive practice. Within this context, the frame is always a figure of arbitrariness. The frame is the figure for the explicit and hidden rules that govern the differential play of any particular discursive practice. That there are rules is not arbitrary. What is arbitrary is the specific set of rules governing any particular discourse or "language game." When the rules are conventional, they are seldom noticed until the singularity of an event issues forth in a series of moves or lines of flight that goes outside of the containment of a frame.

The notion of the singularity, like the notion of the frame, requires definition because it too is a heuristic notion for an experiment in thinking about thinking that does not begin with an identity between thinking and being. We can begin by saying that singularities are aporetic. We cannot get through them or behind them. They are points of intensity, intersections, conjunctions of forces, incorrigibles from which there is an emission of significations or a becoming of a differential play. This is a modest notion of an intellectual, material, or physical state of affairs that is not yet meaningful. It is an attempt to introduce into epistemic reflection another interpretively neutral notion that will pressure the meaning of interpretation. We have experiences of singularities, but we usually do not notice them as singular unless they are anomalous within the frame of current interpretive discourse.

Deleuze says that "the singularity belongs to another dimension than that of denotation, manifestation, or signification." And, in the same paragraph he also says, "singularities are turning points and points of inflection; bottlenecks, knots, foyers, and centers; points of fusion, condensation, and boiling; points of tears and joy, sickness and health, hope and anxiety, 'sensitive' points" (LS, p. 52). Singularities are points of resistance within the interpretive meaning of experience. They are ambivalent since they are not fixed within the frame of their occurrence. The singularity is an event around which thinking recoils. Thinking turns on itself in an experience of inadequacy. The singularity is yet something to be thought and we do not know until it is thought whether it can be thought in the frame of its occurrence. The quote from Deleuze causes us to realize that singularities are those confusions in life that are sometimes fleeting but which can also be a complete breakdown of understanding. The question for rethinking thinking is how to attend to these experiences in the framing of interpretation. Since we are always already within specific discursive practices, singularities will occur within these practices, although their status is of a nature that does not always fit the prevailing practice. That is, an event occurs that can be thought of as singular in the sense that it resists explanation in the current interpretive practice. A new thinking, a new speaking, a new writing flows from the singularity. This new thinking can be within the frame of current interpretive practice, but singular events also can be indexed on multiple registers that are not contained within the frame of prevailing interpretive practices. They are always "other," but these alterities can be empiricities that escape interpretation, heterodoxies that conflict with interpretation, or multiplicities that extend beyond the range of interpretation. Singular events can have the intimacy of a new love affair or a broken love affair and also the generality of cosmic events such as the death of God, the end of history, the closure of the book, and the displacement of the subject. Or, a singularity can be a simple gesture, a metaphor, a juxtaposition of images.

What we know in the encounter with singularities is that there are unsolved riddles that bear on our senses of self and world. We know that familiar definitions of selfhood are too simple to carry the complexities of experience that are part of our witness to life. In particular, the self as an individual and yet universal subjectivity is too much of a voluntaristic fantasy to be credible even in the vagaries of everyday experience. Life is sometimes drunk and sometimes sober, sometimes rich and sometimes poor, sometimes healthy and sometimes sick. The dominant frame of appearances is always unstable if we even only moderately attend to what we experience. Any of our constructed notions of the self simply give way when confronted with exigencies and incorrigibilities of body and mind embedded in a complex nexus of material, physical, and intellectual forces and flows. It is this nexus that is the heterological infrastructure of the subjectivity from which the identity of the self is inscribed. This means that the self is constituted in what is other than self.

Singularities mark aspects of the heterological infrastructure that were or are the excluded "other" in interpretive processes of homogenization, abstraction, or universalization. The reception of singularities into experience can be a doubling phenomenon. On one hand, the singularity destabilizes prevailing interpretive practices. On the other hand, new possibilities and new lines of interpretation issue forth. The question is whether we can intentionally frame a discursive practice that is less resistant to the disclosure of aspects that we have been calling singularities. Ironically, the path to less resistance in postmodern conditions may be a path of resistance to the interpretive hegemony of a pure universal understanding of subjectivity.

The framing of a discourse is the enfranchisement of a voice. Who is speaking? Who do we allow to speak? Who have we not allowed to speak? Liberation and revolution are often about voice, about being allowed to speak. The diverse politics of liberation are not just about politics. They are also about epistemology and, conversely, epistemology is always also about politics.

If we are looking for a guide into this dense world of politics and epistemology, and we usually do need guides when exploring new ways of thinking, perhaps we will again want to turn to Nietzsche, who was historically the paradigmatic philosopher for challenging the Cartesian construct of the self as pure subjectivity. Nietzsche traversed unstable territories of epistemological undecidability and can give us clues as to how we might provisionally frame a discourse of heterogeneities. With Nietzsche we are careful because we have some understanding of how a philosophical project can break down, crack up, and how a philosophical problematic can be dissolved rather than resolved. There are no packaged tours in Nietzsche's thought, no categorical imperatives, and no divine individuation to stabilize surface effects of meaning. There is no guarantee that the self will come home or be resettled.

As Deleuze notes, Nietzsche, as early as *The Birth of Tragedy*, "allowed the *groundless* Dionysus to speak." It, however, was later—after freeing himself from Wagner and Schopenhauer—that "he explored a world of impersonal and pre-individual singularities, a world he then called Dionysian or of the will to power, a free and unbound energy. These are nomadic singularities which are no longer imprisoned within the fixed individuality of the infinite Being [the notorious immutability of God], nor inside the sedentary boundaries of the finite subject [the notorious limits of knowledge]" (LS, p. 107). With Nietzsche, philosophy becomes a transhumant culture. Sense is a Dionysian machine with many lines of flight and multiple configurations and convergences. The logic of sense is not in argument or predication. It is an event of which argument is but one manifestation. In particular, argument and explanation are exfoliations that follow an event. The knowledge of the frame is the aftereffect of a differential play initiated in the singularity of the event. The frame does not always contain the event. The excitement of Nietzsche is that he enfranchised the multiple voices of events so that "the notorious limits of knowledge" were permeable. The danger is that the Dionysian sense machine could become a "Tower of Babel" and lines of differentiation could become randomly disjunctive. There are many surfaces in Nietzsche's thought, so we never know in advance what will be the direction of the line of differentiation that is the aftereffect of a singularity. There may even be multiple lines that traverse different surfaces.

The singularity is part of the differential play that we know as thinking. We might even say that in a heterological infrastructure it is part of the transcendental field, but it is much like a wild card or a floating signifier in the inscription of order. Singularities are in discourse but they are not necessarily generated out of discourse. They can wander through discourse pressuring its constructions. They can wander out of discourse. They can even be turns within discourse. Metaphor, gesture, and meaning are all events.

The problem with trying to define or characterize the singularity is that it is not known directly. We know it by its effects. We know it as it is marked on different registers or recorded on different surfaces. Part of what Nietzsche risked in the enfranchisement of Dionysian voices was the multiplication of registers for the recording of singular events. What he gave up was the unity of apperception that was constituted in the identity of being and thinking. The privilege of consciousness in the assertion of "I think" became an effect alongside of other effects, a secondary process. What he gained was that thinking could not be reduced to pure subjectivity. Thinking gained genealogies.

Singularities are contingencies within thinking. Sometimes in specific turns are they generated out of thinking, although this is usually outside of an intentional structure. However, independent of their originary status, they can be indexed as surface effects in the genealogies of specific thought processes. But, this indexing does not just happen. It is a differential process. The recording surfaces for the inscription of meaning must be interrogated. This is a way that thinking acts upon thinking. The secondary process cathects the primary process and is as such implicated in the primary process. This is a reflexive rather than reflective event. This process is still a framing but what is framed is a problematic interrogative surface. Thinking can initiate meaning when it allows its discourse to trouble itself.

The surface is a figuration in discourse to designate where thinking appears or shows itself. Thinking has to come to some expression or we are not yet thinking. The metaphor of a recording surface is an acknowledgment of the necessity of material expression in the constitution of an event. There are all kinds of machines for the distribution and differentiation of space and sound in the expression of thinking that define recording surfaces. These machines enable a semiotic process and generate lines of differentiation. Speaking, writing, gesturing, and fashion are differential. Paper, the body, cloth, and sound are recording surfaces. Thinking invests in itself when it prepares surfaces and modes of differentiation for marking surfaces.

There are many remarkable machines for spacing and differentiation: the tongue, hands, the alphabet, grammar, numbers, dictionaries. Learning languages is the becoming of thinking. There are many languages and within languages there are marginal grammars and minority literatures that constitute, complicate, and extend possibilities for thinking. What needs to be marked and constantly remarked in thinking about thinking is that machines of differentiation are material and have histories. There is no natural *tabula rasa* that is a recording surface for pure thinking. Languages have histories. Words have etymologies. Voices modulate with age.

If Wittgenstein is correct in stating that the meaning of a word is its use in language, it also needs to be stated that *use* is not fixed.[3] Certainly there are ordinary uses of a word, but there can also be extraordinary uses that are important in thinking about thinking. This is especially important when singularities mark the recording surface of thinking. It is the singularity that needs to be thought. Singularities include the knots and intensities in our lives. They remain "other" unless they can be thought.

It would appear that in the shallowness of secular culture there are singularities that this culture has not been able to think—that is why we have raised the question of whether we need to think theologically even in a secular culture. Is there anything special on the surfaces or in the mechanics of theological text production that are differential possibilities for thickening the meaning of secular lives? Has the silencing of theology diminished the capacity for living? This is not a meaningless question for those who are restless with their sense of boredom or emptiness.

The question is whether theology as a discursive practice differs in any important way from other discursive practices. In a remarkable quotation from one of the appendices of Deleuze's *The Logic of Sense,* he says: "It is our epoch which has discovered theology. One no longer needs to believe in God. We seek rather the 'structure,' that is, the form which may be filled with beliefs, but the structure has no need to be filled in order to be called 'theological.' Theology is now the science of nonexisting entities, the manner in which these entities—divine or anti-divine, Christ or Antichrist—animate language and make for it this glorious body which is divided into disjunctions. Nietzsche's prediction about the link between God and grammar has been realized" (LS, p. 281). Can we make sense out of what appears to be an outrageous claim?

In one sense, we have already conceded to Nietzsche's link between God and grammar by thinking of theology first of all as a

---

3. Ludwig Wittgenstein, *Philosophical Investigations,* translated by G. E. M. Anscombe (Oxford: Basil Blackwell, 1967).

discursive practice. The question that remains is whether theological practice animates language and makes for it a "glorious body?" If belief is removed from the hermeneutical circle, certainly a common understanding of theology has been transgressed. But, we would expect a Nietzschean theology to be uncommon because he has already made space for the voice of Dionysus. Other spaces need to be made. The population of religious figurations is immense. The are lives of saints, voices of prophets, icons, sacraments, creeds, narratives, rituals, monks, rabbis, and the list could go on for pages. These entities and figurations are part of the theological recording surface, the body on which a theological practice will be marked. More simply, the surface for a theological discursive practice is the whole of religious tradition and history. This surface will be a heterogeneous space mixing entities and nonentities. It will bear the markings of languages of the miraculous, of confession, and of avowal, as well as of positivist history.

This surface is topologically complex. Its planes, lines, curvatures, and spacings are emergent and its texture is subject to alteration and cultivation. This is part of the meaning of theological text production. The field of the theological surface is already richly textured. It is also in a state of becoming, and the specificity for points of access to the theological surface depends on the localization of our discourse. Bhakti ritual practice, the dreams of desert saints, or systematic theology have no natural privilege over each other as points of access. It depends on where we are.

Beginnings are contingent and, as suggested, singular. Lines of differentiation emitted from singularities will sometimes intersect the theological surface. The question is whether these points of intersection can be recognized as points of access to theological thinking. That is, this intersection can be its own singularity, an event that gives rise to thinking on a richly and densely populated surface.

There, however, also can be a nonrecognition of points of intersection. Then the event is isolated. There is silence. This is not a primordial or mystical silence. This is the silence of an isolated event, a crack or fissure in discourse. It is important but meaningless until it is brought into another discursive practice. It is a wound that does not bleed until it is made visible and marked as a silence. Marking silences will be one of the tasks of postmodern theology. These can be silences even in what has been traditionally thought of as theology. The recognition of these points of intersection requires some framing of the theological surface, some designation of the theological field. By simply surveying the surface of the history of religions we encounter some intellectual constructions that make demands on the framing of a theological surface. The Muslims' claim that Allah is "Lord of the Worlds,"[4] the litany of identifications of Brahman with all that there is in the *Bhagavad Gita*,[5] or Tillich's identification of faith with ultimate concern[6] are all examples of pressure on framing theological discourse to characterize its surface as unconditional. Nothing in principle is excluded from interrogation and elaboration. This is what is meant by saying that the theological surface is interrogative and problematic. Whatever is marked on this surface is interrogated by its relationship to figurations of ultimacy, extremity, and unconditionality. The surface is cultivated by a rhetoric of interrogation.

The claim of unconditionality might make us first think that this theological surface is a metaphysical surface and that through a sleight-of-hand we have returned to ontotheology. It may seem that what I am saying is that what needs to be thought is the unthought relationship of beings to Being because of the unconditionality of Being. In fact, this is a strategy I want to avoid because, if privileged over other discursive practices, I think it can lead to an occultation of thought and a paralyzing of theological thinking. If privileged, an ontological frame of interpretation generates its own stream of forgetfulness.

Since we cannot think Being-itself, "thinking" being a differential process, the ontological surface is constituted by saying Being.

---

4. See Richard Cragg, *The House of Islam* (Belmont, CA: Dickenson Publishing Co., 1969), chap. 1.

5. *The Song of God: Bhagavad Gita*, translated by Swami Prabhavananda and Christopher Isherwood (New York: New American Library, 1951), pp. 67, 79–82, 88–90.

6. Paul Tillich, *The Dynamics of Faith* (New York: Harper & Row, 1957), p. 1.

Being is a single voice. "The univocity of Being does not mean that there is one and the same Being; on the contrary, beings are multiple and different, they are always produced by a disjunctive synthesis, and they themselves are disjointed and divergent, *membra disjuncta*. The univocity of Being signifies that Being is Voice that it is said, and that it is said in one and the same 'sense' of everything about which it is said" (LS, p. 179). What is forgotten is difference. What are forgotten are singularities. Being absorbs beings, homogenizes thought, and divests itself too quickly of specificities.

The metaphysical/ontological surface intersects with the theological surface but it does not constitute it. Ontology is a complementary discursive practice but it has no privilege over politics, economics, history, theology, or any other discursive practice. It, however, does pressure other discursive practices as it intersects with them. It transgresses the closure of other discursive practices by valencing the unthought within thought. The unthought traverses other surfaces of thinking as a floating signifier and makes them always incomplete and unresolvable. Thus, metaphysics and ontology disturb but do not subsume other discourses.

What I am suggesting is that speaking the univocity of Being resists cultivation into a diverse enough surface for an adequate distribution of what we have been calling singularities. Metaphysics and ontology are instead transgressive discourses to be allied with theology in the cultivation of its surface. This audacious claim is possible only because the metaphysical realm of essences was replaced by the transcendental field, conditions of possibility, in Enlightenment philosophy and has further been replaced by a quasi-transcendental field, rules for the formation of discourse, since the various "linguistic turns" in recent philosophies.[7] Not only has discourse come to be privileged in philosophical analyses, but the various hermeneutics of suspicion have complicated representation in discourse with a pervasive sense of equivocation. It is difficult to persist in the development

---

7. See Rodolph Gasché, *The Tain of the Mirror: Derrida and the Philosophy of Reflection* (Cambridge: Harvard University Press, 1986), for the notion of quasi-transcendental conditions.

of a metaphysical discourse in which the "Univocity of Being" is an equivocal notion, sometimes philosophical, sometimes psychological, sometimes political in its connectedness and in its entailments. Metaphysical and ontological discourses are special rhetorics and can in this sense be used as parts of a rhetorical strategy in the cultivation of a theological surface. Critical philosophy's privileging of discourse as an object of analysis has as a complement the privileging of rhetoric in synthetic construction. I say this to emphasize that the strategies for the cultivation of a theological surface are themselves rhetorical. The tools are tools of rhetorical figuration.

Since there are many rhetorical strategies their relative adequacy will have to be measured by their usefulness in relating to the task at hand, the cultivation of a theological surface for the complicating and deepening of secular consciousness in theological discourse. Since this task is valenced in both secular and religious experience, convergences will be necessary for its development. There will need to be lines of convergence for the distribution of images, concepts, and singularities. The development of these lines is the cultivation of the theological surface. This is a texturing of a space of inscription.

Because there are always at least two perspectival lines of differentiation that will converge, there will always be some form of a dialectical element in the process. In the preparatory work for theological text production I think it is helpful to make explicit the understanding of the dialectical strategy that is being used. We need not assume that a dialectical process will always be oppositional and antithetical.

We have earlier discussed metaphorical strategies that have a dialectical element in the convergence of dissimilars, but in the cultivation of a theological surface I want instead to emphasize a metonymical strategy for a dialectical triangulation. What I am suggesting is that two discursive practices be brought into intimate proximity with each other, forcing metonymical contiguity and thus be able to pressure each other.

The advantage of this strategy is that one of the discursive practices can be explicitly theological and the other can be explicitly secular. The secular discourse can be a familiar habitation outside of any hermeneutical circle that presupposes belief. The secular discourse is a point of access to a theological process.

The theological discourse is allowed to speak in its own terms. It doesn't have to become less than itself to be part of a dialectical process. The dialectic does not require dialogue. The two practices speak but not explicitly to each other.

The dynamic presupposition of this dialectical model is that thinking as a discursive practice is not clear and distinct and is not a clean, well-lit space. As suggested earlier, a figure for the rootedness of a discursive practice will resemble more a rhizome than a taproot of knowledge. There will be stems of exploration and lines of filiation that both spread and are frustrated in the subsoil of experience.[8] The heterological infrastructure of a discursive practice is not contained by the economy of its representational surface. The nexus of forces, fluxes, pulsions, and materiality that are originating conditions for both discursive practices forced into dialectical proximity will cross, intersect, reinforce, and frustrate each other, thus producing surface effects and cultivating a new surface. This process neither precludes nor presupposes that the surface economies of the two discursive practices interpenetrate each other, although it would be unlikely that there would be no contact since the dialectical strategy is an experimental and intentional secondary process of thinking.

What is presupposed is that comingling of primary processes will usually have surface effects. The risk in this strategy is that we do not know what these effects will be prior to their expression. Neither discursive practice can be guaranteed its stability. A metonymically structured dialectic is an experiment in intensification. If life were already sufficiently intense and satisfying, we probably would not be willing to take the risk.

This, however, does not seem to be the way we experience our lives. The recordings of our individual lives have often been a cataloging of the oppression by ordinariness. The recordings of our collective lives have been a cataloging of profound political, social, and economic injustices in the midst of remarkable technological achieve-

8. See footnote 5 in chapter 2.

ments. The twentieth century has been a vast web of incongruities. There is a sense of disaster, but we do not yet know how to write or speak the disaster. We can fail to notice or fail to exfoliate the meaning of a gesture at a swimming pool that comes to be known as Agnes. There are many of these gestures that are squandered in our experience. We have also failed to notice or have been unable or unwilling to exfoliate the meaning of Smyrna 1922, the Holocaust, Hiroshima, the war in Vietnam, Sandinistas, famine in the Sudan, the homeless of New York. The rhetoric of "Desert Storm" is not adequate to the death of coalition soldiers or to the sufferings of the Iraqi people. We are not even able to count the deaths in "Desert Storm." In general, our narrative capacities have not been equal to the demands of the events of our individual and collective lives. We have to risk new strategies for thinking if we simply attend to our experience. The surfaces of too many of our discursive practices have been too simple and too uniform to bear the markings of diverse forces of desire, love, justice, injustice and space differential play for the exfoliation of meaning of the diverse events we have been calling singularities. Experience is too often diminished by regularizing the recording surfaces of discourses in an attempt to achieve familiarity and security.

There are many examples closely akin to the dialectical strategy that I am proposing for the cultivation of a theological surface even though they are not always self-consciously experimental dialectics. One of the most obvious of these examples is the juxtaposition of personal narrative development with the discursive practices of the arts. What are we doing when we read a novel, listen to music, or visit galleries and museums? We are probably doing a lot of things, since these are highly overdetermined events, but, intentionally or unintentionally, we are bringing two or more diverse discursive practices into close proximity with each other. We are crossing genealogies and risking a mix of generative primary processes. Since the surface of subjective inscription is always in a process of elaborative becoming it can be expected that there will be surface effects from these activities. We don't ask if a novel or symphony is true. We ask if our reading or listening experience is important, meaningful, or intense. That is, does this experience have surface effects? Does it elaborate the surface of subjective inscription?

Not only is the surface of subjective inscription altered, the text that is read is misread in a strong reading. The text that is read is also marked by the surface of effects of mixing primary processes. I think that this is why Harold Bloom is correct in understanding the tropes in a map of misreading as defense mechanisms that are a part of primary repression.[9]

When the surface effects are vague or nonobservable in either register of inscription, the experience does not seem important. Literature, music, or the visual arts can be a confirmation of the ordinary. This, however, is a judgment that cannot be made in advance of reading, listening, and seeing and it cannot be universalized because discursive genealogies are always specific. We don't know in advance who will be reading a text and when and where it will be read.

The example from the arts was used because I think that is readily accessible. We could have used any accessible discursive practice over against narrative subjectivity to illustrate characteristics of this dialectical process. However, when we turn to theology, I am not suggesting that theological texts always be read in direct juxtaposition with narrative subjectivity. I am suggesting a method of indirection or mediation. Theological texts need to be read in juxtaposition with other texts that are already accessible in a secular culture. Theology as a discursive practice can be read against (next to) literature as a discursive practice, or against psychoanalysis as a discursive practice, or against ideology critique as a discursive practice, or against critical theory as a discursive practice. These are ways that I am suggesting that the theological surface be cultivated and prepared for readings that are investments in the formations of new subjectivities.

Traditional theologies can be read against critical theories, feminist theories, or ideology critiques, thus cultivating surfaces for radical theologies. Social texts can be read against radical theologies, thus cultivating surfaces for liberation theologies. There can be an ongo-

9. Harold Bloom, *The Anxiety of Influence* (New York: Oxford University Press, 1973) and *The Map of Misreading* (New York: Oxford University Press, 1975).

ing multiplication of theological surfaces. This is a primary meaning for postmodern theological text production. Theological surfaces can be prepared so that subjectivity can be interwoven with theological heterologies, inscribed on surfaces that have theological genealogies. These will be thick surfaces that can be marked with deep inscriptions.

Six

Theological Surfaces: Heterology, Ontology, and Eschatology

> The name of this infinite and inexhaustible depth and ground of all
> being is God. That depth is what the word God means.
>
> Paul Tillich, *The Shaking of the Foundations* (p. 57)

> The silent embarrassment of using the divine name can protect us
> against violating the divine mystery.
>
> Paul Tillich, *The Eternal Now* (p. 98)

> Revelation is not information about divine things; it is the ecstatic man-
> ifestation of the Ground of Being in events persons and things. Such
> manifestations have shaking, transforming, and healing power.
>
> Paul Tillich, *Systematic Theology II* (p. 166)

These quotations from Paul Tillich concerning the divine name
mark insights that reveal both a claim and a tension in his theological thinking. The name of God must be both spoken and
unspoken in the theological peregrinations that plumb life's mys-
teries and wander through the labyrinth of life's complexities. The
same name functions to disclose and conceal, comes into speech and
resists speech, and, giving rise to discursive practices in which the
symbol is a symptom, is a donation of meaning that is critically
implicated in its own self-emptying. It is this tension, so artfully
inscribed along the many boundaries of Tillich's systematic theological explorations, occasional writings and sermons, that I want to
consider in relationship to the notion of surface preparation in theological text production.

Tillich is not a postmodern theologian. He clearly works within
the ontotheological tradition. The hermeneutical strategies within
his thinking are elaborative rather than deconstructive. Yet, his theology has spoken meaningfully to many within a secular culture as
well as to those who have defined themselves in a religious culture.

I want to suggest that the efficacy of his thinking within a secular milieu is in part attributable to the cultivation of a complicated and variegated textual surface on which there can be inscribed diverse singularities and multiplicities of secular life. A theological surface for Tillich would be satisfying only if it were a surface of the deep. "Why have men [*sic*] always asked for the truth? Is it because they have been disappointed with the surfaces, and have known that the truth which does *not* disappoint dwells below the surfaces in the depth?"[1] Tillich entertains figurations of ultimacy, extremity, and unconditionality on the theological surface that constitutes a meaning of depth.

Tillich's method of correlation and correspondent answering theology makes his work continually subject to reformulations of the philosophical problematic and also subject to cultural change. To work in the tradition of Tillich's apologetic task is to accept this challenge. Since Tillich's theology is so thoroughly interwoven with philosophical formulations, alterations of the philosophical thread in his thinking will change the substance of his theology and continually alter the texture of its surface. These changes, although fundamental, extend rather than abandon his theological project.

His specific philosophical indebtedness to the ontotheological tradition of nineteenth-century German idealism and more general mortgage to the autonomous subject of Cartesianism are allied with a theological exigency in his thinking that subverts and transcends the totalization and exclusivity of these philosophical traditions. The philosophical tradition is strained when it comes to theological articulation. It is along resultant fault lines that cracks and fissures are markings of forces that resist explication and in their alterity are proper concerns for theological interrogation. That is, the theological development of a philosophical tradition can disturb and sometimes uproot that tradition to which it is indebted. Theological thinking is not supplemental to philosophical inquiry, but theology is implicated in the formation of discursive practices so that its for-

---

1. Paul Tillich, *The Shaking of the Foundations* (New York: Charles Scribner's Sons, 1948), p. 53. Hereafter cited in the text as SF with appropriate page numbers.

mal criteria have a quasi-transcendental relationship with the discursive theological achievement.

In the first volume of *Systematic Theology,* Tillich defines two formal criteria for theology. The first formal criterion is: "The object of theology is what concerns us ultimately. Only those propositions are theological which deal with their object insofar as it can become a matter of ultimate concern for us."[2] This criterion functions as an interrogative demand and implicates theology in existential value decisions. The second formal criterion is descriptive rather than interrogative and is philosophical rather than theological. "Our ultimate concern is that which determines our being or not-being. Only those statements are theological which deal with their object insofar as it can become a matter of being or not-being for us" (ST, 1:14). The lines of filiation for the second criterion are in the Western ontotheological tradition and, although it is an elaboration of the first criterion, it is neither a condition for it or the only possible elaboration of it.

The status of these criteria differ. The first criterion instantiates a question and defines the scale of inquiry. The second criterion is a strategic implementation of the first criterion in a specific discursive situation. The demands of scale in the first criterion exceed the specific and localized achievement in the articulated working out of the second criterion. What I want to suggest is that, while the second criterion can be formulated without faulting the first criterion, the formulation of the first criterion cannot be contained within the range of articulation of the second criterion and subverts any totalization of the second criterion.

This suggestion does not undo any of the achievement of Tillich's systematic theological reflections. It merely marks a tension in that achievement that is important if we seek to direct his thinking outside of the containment of the Western ontotheological tradition. This is a desideratum for a contemporary reading of Tillich's theology for two reasons.

---

2. Paul Tillich, *Systematic Theology,* 3 vols. (Chicago: University of Chicago Press, 1951, 1957, 1963), vol. 1, p. 12. Hereafter cited in the text as ST with appropriate volume and page numbers.

The first is that, as often noted in this book, the ontotheological tradition has been diagnosed as not being in good health. We can again refer to Mark Taylor, in his book *Erring: A Postmodern A\theology,* explicitly arguing that there are four losses that confront any postmodern theological inquiry: (1) the death of God, (2) the disappearance or displacement of the self, (3) the end of history, and (4) the closure of the book. The interdependence of the concepts of God, self, history, and book means that the death, disappearance, end, or closure of any of these concepts would have implications that can be traced through the dissemination of the others. Although it was the proclamation of the death of God by Nietzsche's madman sustained throughout the vagaries of twentieth-century American theology that has received the most theological attention, the Hegelian achievement and its deconstruction have deracinated the autonomy and force of concepts of self, history, and book. Confidence in a categorical agreement with being has been undermined by what remained unthought in its most elaborate philosophical expressions, which was followed by a history of abjection in which what was unthought and unthinkable in social and political life has become commonplace. There has been a shaking of the foundations that demands more than a reconstruction under the aegis of the ontotheological tradition.

The second reason why it is desirable to give priority to Tillich's first formal criterion is the unfulfilled promise in some of his later work toward the development of a theology of the history of religions that could have family resemblances with a secular postmodern theology. In *Christianity and the Encounter with World Religions,* Tillich defined religion in correlation with the first formal criterion of theology. "Religion is the state of being grasped by an ultimate concern, a concern which qualifies all other concerns as preliminary and which itself contains the answer to the question of the meaning of our life."[3] He also acknowledges that "revelation" is always received in the context of a finite human situation.[4] This means that religions are always

3. Paul Tillich, *Christianity and the Encounter with World Religions* (Chicago: University of Chicago Press, 1963), p. 4. Hereafter cited in the text as CWR with appropriate page numbers.
4. Paul Tillich, *The Future of Religions* (Chicago: University of Chicago Press, 1966), p. 81. Hereafter cited in the text as FR with appropriate page numbers.

concrete and particular. The "concrete spirit" of religions abides in a tension between their particular manifestations and the qualification of ultimacy. It is the qualification of ultimacy that Tillich can carry over from Christian theology to a theology of the history of religions. However, this is a theological question and not a theological answer, and it is a question that is unformulated in any meaningful way until it is formulated within the discursive practices of the community in which it is asked. This means that within a theology of the religion of the concrete spirit, the "fight of God against religion within religion" is a localized affair (FR, p. 88). He says that "the universal religious basis is the experience of the Holy within the finite," but this does not give us a universal religion or a synthetic mixture of religions (FR, p. 86). "A mixture of religions destroys in each of them the concreteness which gives it its dynamic power" (CWR, p. 96). A theology of the history of religions can be no less than an intertextual interlacing of heterogeneities set against a claim or horizon of ultimacy.

It is only within the specific discursive practices of a community that criteria for the articulation of an ultimate concern can have any meaning. As Tillich himself suggests, "words are the result of the encounter of the human mind with reality" (ST, 2:19). That is, what comes to mind and what we have in mind in the encounter with reality are words. There is a privileging of the formation of discourse in this suggestion. If the encounter with reality gives us *words,* then *words* are going to be the markings indexing our experience of the *real.* A further implication of this suggestion is that criteria governing theological or philosophical thinking are rules for the formation of discursive practices. This does not mean that there is nothing outside of textuality, but it does mean that our thinking is always textual. Concepts are achievements of the differential interplay of words and have their status in the general textuality of thinking. Discourse is the cultural register for reality.

This would suggest that the *question* of being has no status outside of discourse and, if we are to understand Tillich's second criterion for theological thinking, we will need to examine his use of the word *being* in the specificity of his discursive practices. Is his use of the word *being* such that this use would be invariant across all other specific discourses? Is there a word *being* or its equivalent in all discursive practices that can function nonsymbolically inside of the differential structure of text production as an absolute point of reference? If not, the second criterion is not an exigency of all theological thinking but is a specifically located articulation of the first criterion. There is little question that Tillich thinks that "Being is the basic absolute."[5] He means more than the word *being*, but of course his talk is about the word *being*. He says that there are two concepts of being. One is the result of a radical abstraction and radical negation. Being means "not being anything particular, simply being" (MSA, p. 81). This concept is an empty absolute and arrests any clarification beyond its assertion. It would be no more than a null point in any discourse.

His other conceptual usage is negatively and positively experiential in its several moments. The negative experience is the shock of non-being. He is asserting that non-being is as basic as being and that the awareness of possible non-being is experienced as a state of anxiety.[6] The shock of non-being can be as simple as the practical experience of having to die (MSA, p. 82). The economy of death is assimilated by Tillich into the language of being and non-being and interwoven with guilt, condemnation, emptiness, and meaninglessness.

The positive experience is the experience of *eros*, which Tillich says is the love of being and then likens it to Augustine's *amor amoris* [love of love] and Spinoza's *amor intellectualis* [intellectual love] (MSA, p. 82). He calls this love "a feeling for the holiness of being as being, whatever it may be" (MSA, p. 82). This being is an infinitely full but indefinite absolute. Here, the economy of love is assimilated by Tillich into the language of being and interwoven with all particularities without being identified with any of them.

5. Paul Tillich, *My Search for Absolutes* (New York: Simon and Schuster, 1967), p. 81. Hereafter cited in the text as MSA with appropriate page numbers.
6. Paul Tillich, *The Courage To Be* (New Haven: Yale University Press, 1952), pp. 32, 35. Hereafter cited in the text as CB with appropriate page numbers.

We might ask if the language of being and non-being add any-thing to the textual economies of life and death. Or, do the languages of life and death add anything to the concept of being? As a concept, does *being* mean anything more as an infinitely full but indefinite absolute than as "not being anything particular, simply being?" It would appear that the concept of being has been filled by its associa-tion with love and death, but we need at least to suspect that it is the word *being* that is here referenced in the differential play of specific texts. That is, being is implicated in a play of differences rather than having the play of differences implicated in being. The move through languages of life and death does not draw us closer to an experience of being. For example, the love of love or the anxiety before the awareness of death do not witness to being and non-being unless being and non-being are privileged as signifiers that are interchange-able with all other signifiers in chains of signification. It is not the lan-guages of love or death that speak being, but it is the possibility for grafting the ontotheological tradition onto these languages that is witnessed in the philosophical appropriation of these discourses. Tillich does not distinguish the framing of a discourse from its inter-nal economy or external milieu.

The framing of Tillich's discourses on religion is philosophical; to understand and assess the applicability of his work outside of the scene of its origination, we must account for the frame in its materi-ality, spacing, thickness, and double-edged qualities. Frames delin-eate a contrast between figure and ground, inside and outside. The ambiguity of framing is a trait of its thickness and double edges. From the inside of a discourse the internal edge of the frame is the point of contrast between the figure and ground so that the frame belongs to the ground. The frame is thus naturalized so that its struc-ture appears to be the structure of the ground giving prominence to the specific figures of discourse. From the outside of a discourse, the external edge of the frame is the point of contrast between the figure and the ground so that the materiality and structure of the frame appear to be internal to the specific figures of discourse.

This means that if the frame of a discourse is the ontotheological tradition, then from the outside it would appear that a specific discourse is implicated in being and non-being without ever being explicitly ontological and from the inside it would appear that the discourse is grounded in the structure of being and non-being without being explicitly ontological. By reciprocally shifting perspectives between inside and outside, the thickness of the frame is erased in a double naturalization so that there is the presence of an uncanny trace of what is absent in the actual figures of discourse. Reason must always go outside of itself to incorporate its own frame whether its perspective is from the inside or outside of a particular discursive situation. This is one reading of Tillich's claim that "ecstasy is fulfilled, not denied, rationality" (ST, 2:76).

The philosophical frame of Tillich's thinking is transcendental. He regards philosophical inquiry as an investigation of "the character of the general structures that make experience possible" (ST, 1:19). These structures are ontological, but they are marked on an epistemological register. "Reality as such, or reality as a whole, is not the whole of reality; it is the structure which makes reality a whole and therefore a potential object of knowledge" and "subjective reason is the structure of mind which enables it to grasp and shape reality" (ST, 1:18, 76).

It is here that we see one of the important tensions in the formulation of Tillich's thought. Subjective reason has an experiential primacy in that it is what grasps and shapes reality but it is reality as such that makes reality a potential object of knowledge. This is a complex dialectic. "Self-relatedness is implied in every experience. There is something that 'has' and something that is 'had,' and the two are one" (ST, 1:169). It is subjective reason that constructs ontological concepts, but "the truth of all ontological concepts is their power of expressing that which makes the subject-object structure possible. They constitute this structure; they are not controlled by it" (ST, 1:169). Subjective reason constructs the conceptual structure by which it is constituted. It would appear that subjectivity is displaced by its own achievement and that reason has subverted its autonomy.

The paradox of the philosophy of reflection is that the subject can only know itself as an object. This becoming other than itself to know itself leaves a remainder. The mirroring of subjective reflection arrests the mirroring in its objectification so that it cannot include the mirror's mirroring. Subjectivity can only be known in the space of its objective inscription which is other than itself. But, as Tillich notes, it is here that the identity of subjectivity is constituted, which means that its identity is deferred and belated. The priority and autonomy of subjectivity are lost in its necessarily impure reflection. What this means is that we cannot privilege an ontological conceptual structure on the basis of a pure reflection of subjectivity because that ontological conceptual structure subverts the priority of the subject by constituting the conditions of its possibility. However we traverse a philosophy of reflection between ontology and epistemology, its inquiry is convoluted by the force of its own transcendental questions. Wherever we begin the inquiry, the determinations of epistemological or ontological identities are in the linguistic register of the other field of inquiry. This is a circle that cannot ground itself and its moments are heterogeneous. Neither epistemological nor ontological concepts are determinate in themselves. Their fundamental concepts have an internal undecidability or incompleteness that resists their universalization or naturalization in a general system.

This recognition works against Tillich's confidence that with language we have universals which liberate us from bondage to concrete situations (ST, 1:31). Without a truly autonomous discourse our thinking is always situated and it is always on a surface. Transcendental philosophy does not have a domain that is proper to itself. It does not resolve itself in epistemological or ontological categories. It is always implicated in alterities that it cannot determine from its own determinate standpoint. It can be a frame for other inquiries but it cannot privilege itself as a universal frame because of the heterogeneity of the alterities in which it is implicated. The philosophical frame of Tillich's theological inquiries is partitioned and marked by its own undecidability.

The line of my argument can be summarized by noting two of its implications. The first is that the formation of Tillich's philosophical discourse reciprocally traverses the relationship between the conflicting primacies of epistemology and ontology and disestablishes the autonomy of any proper domain from which philosophy can assert a universal privilege in the formation of other discursive practices. The second implication is that without a proper domain that has universal meaning, ontology is a heterological supplement to a transcendental interrogation of specific and concrete discourses.

This means that philosophy cannot come to closure in its own articulation and, more important for our reflections, it does not justify closure in the theological discourses that it frames. The weaving of heterological discourses into theological discourses, even when these discourses approximate expressions of wholeness and totality, should leave traces of their origination in seams and fissures on the surface of the theological text. That is, there should be fissures in dominant theological figurations revealing lines of force or traces of alterity that cannot be contained within this discursive practice. These fissures will mark strains not only at the periphery of thought and thereby be only a matter of secondary concern—they will mark strains at the center of thought. For example, in Tillich's theology, it is *being* that "remains the content, the mystery and eternal *aporia* of thinking" (ST, 2:11). It is *being* that dominates his theological discourse and it is *being* that bears the mark of the heterogeneity constitutive of his philosophical discourse.

In a rather remarkable and subtle formulation, Tillich makes an incision in being with the question of God that qualifies his understanding of a homogeneous concept of being. He seeks to develop the question of God *as* the question implied in being (ST, 1:166). This is not the same as saying that the question of God is implied in the question of being. "It is the finitude of being that drives us to the question of God" (ST, 1:166). It would appear that the question of God is not contained in the question of being and no simple identity is possible.

This statement would seem to be contradicted by Tillich's identification of the being of God with being-itself. He very explicitly says that: "The statement that God is being-itself is a nonsymbolic statement. It does not point beyond itself. It means what it says directly and properly" (ST, 1:238). He also says that "after this has been said, nothing else can be said about God as God which is not symbolic"

(ST, 1:239). As soon as we move to the symbolic register, all of Tillich's formulations of God fissure the nonsymbolic statement that "the being of God is being-itself."

For example, naming God the "living God" is a denial of God as a pure identity of being as being (ST, 1:242). The Trinitarian identification of the first principle of the Godhead as the inexhaustible ground of being is a heterological complication of a pure identity with being. In *The Dynamics of Faith*, Tillich says that "God is a symbol for God."[7] It is the element of the unconditional that constitutes divinity in the idea of God (DF, p. 10). It is always judgment from the priority of the first criterion of theological thinking that gives theological meaning to the second criterion. "The content of absolute faith is the 'God above God'" (CB, p. 182). These are all highly dialectical—heterological—concepts. They are not unlike the speculative formulations that Tillich brings to our attention in Boehme (*Urgrund*), Schopenhauer (will), Nietzsche (will to power), Freud, Hartmann (the unconscious), Bergson (*elan vital*), Scheler, and Jung (strife). These are concepts that are not to be taken conceptually (ST, 1:179). This oxymoronic state of affairs denies privilege to the copula of being.

This means that we recognize that nonconceptual concepts do not function to establish identities. They function in the symbolic realm. This recognition has not always brought about the radical rethinking of theological strategies that we might have expected from the introduction of nonconceptual concepts into our thinking and the consequent move into the symbolic realm. It would appear that the "is" of "being" often functions metaphorically in the symbolic realm, following patterns of analogy and establishing likenesses between dissimilars. When metaphor dominates the rhetoric of theology, the articulations of nonconceptual concepts can approximate nonsymbolic statements in their formal expressions while bracketing any literal claims about reality.

I would like to suggest that the move toward an exclusively

---

7. Paul Tillich, *The Dynamics of Faith* (New York: Harper Torchbooks, 1958), p. 46. Hereafter cited in the text as DF with appropriate page numbers.

metaphorical understanding of theological formulations is a slippage into a postcritical naivete that is too easily accommodated with a precritical naivete. What is obscured by the copula *is* is the radically disjunctive and wholly other demand of the "God above God" on any discourse. A discourse is intruded upon and defamiliarized by unconditional formulations and claims of ultimacy. We cannot gain our footing on the familiar ground of nonsymbolic ontological propositions because we have been forced into the symbolic realm by the internal undecidability of those same propositions. Root ontological concepts also function nonconceptually. It appears that all of the dominant concepts in Tillich's theology function so radically that their juxtaposition in discourse is metonymical rather than properly metaphorical. The disenfranchised copula of being does not establish identities but instead marks a space within a discourse for figurations of ultimacy, thereby further texturing the surface for theological inscription. These nonliteral formulations pressure the discourse and alter its general economy. The discourse is implicated in ultimacy, and even if it is not ontological it is theological.

Tillich certainly thought that there is a final revelation that has the power of negating its particularity without losing itself. This notion depends on the transparency of the *is* in nonsymbolic statements or metaphorical configurations. His own radical formulations for God work against this privilege of the *is*. His use of the *is* is more closely associated in practice with forcing a metonymical alignment of the ordinary with formulations and qualifications of unconditional and ultimate concern. This is why he could turn to a theology of the concrete spirit. He consistently affirmed that "the ultimate can be actual only through the concrete," and "this is the reason why the idea of God has a history" (ST, 1:218).

This history has not come to an end. Tillich can continue to speak to this history because his theological practice was denied closure by the first criterion by which it was established. The explication of the first criterion makes it very clear that the surface for theological inscription is a symbolic register. By pushing theology into the domain of the symbolic, Tillich has intentionally or unintentionally shifted the focus of transcendental inquiry from the quest for foundations to the development of genealogies. We cannot get beyond or beneath the *aporia* of the nonsymbolic statement that God is being-itself. Since it does not point beyond itself, it resists interrogation. It cannot ground or constitute theological discourse. It simply instantiates a negativity within a discourse.

The status of this negativity needs to be assessed within an understanding of symbolic discourse. In *The Dynamics of Faith,* Tillich points out four characteristics of the symbol that will mark the formation of a symbolic discourse. The first is that the symbol points beyond itself (DF, p. 41). Second, unlike a sign, the symbol participates in the reality toward which it points. Third, the symbol "opens up levels of reality which otherwise are closed for us." And, fourth, the symbol unlocks dimensions of ourselves that correspond to the levels of reality that have been opened up (DF, p. 42).

The symbol functions in such a way that it uses the concrete material of ordinary experience and both affirms and negates the ordinary meaning of these concrete experiences. "Every religious symbol negates itself in its literal meaning, but it affirms itself in its self-transcending meaning" (ST, 2:9). Religious symbols pressure theological discourse. "They are directed toward the infinite which they symbolize *and* toward the finite through which they symbolize it. They force the infinite down to finitude and the finite up to infinity" (ST, 1:240).

These characterizations of the symbol and descriptions of the symbolic function are important in analyzing theological discourse, but they do not give us an assessment of the status of the symbol in this discourse. How does the symbol point and participate in the reality it symbolizes? How does the symbol open up new levels of reality and unlock corresponding dimensions of reality in ourselves? How does the symbol *force* the infinite down and the finite up?

We can see the process of the symbolic function perhaps most clearly in the extremities of Tillich's eschatology. Symbolic force is here of particular importance because his eschatology is a praxis of deliverance, a discourse of shaking, transforming, and healing power. Since this discourse is nonliteral and highly symbolic, it is an excellent place to access the general possibilities and conditions of the formation of the symbolic within Tillich's theology. The figurations of eschatology pressure easy resolutions of the status of discourse and its existential valences in the development of his theology. If Tillich's eschatology is wholly symbolic, these questions of the status and efficacy of the symbolic must be addressed as we explicate and assess his eschatological vision. One direction of inquiry would be to affirm a "participation mystique" between the materiality of the symbol and the reality toward which it points. If we could make such an affirmation, it would seem that the symbol could stand alone in a mantic reverie, unlocking doors to reality. This does not seem to be the case. The *forcing* power of the symbolic seems to reside in the differential play of a discourse and not in an ontological mystery.

It is not even clear what we would mean by an ontological mystery, nor is there any obvious experience that we could point to that would give us more than the ontic materiality of the symbol. What we do have are symbol-laden texts. There are symbols embedded in discursive practices and they are the material for a general reflection on a theory of the symbolic.

The concept of a discursive practice is both more modest and more comprehensive than are those of ontology or theology. It is more modest because it stays within itself in a reflexive referentiality and it is more comprehensive because it is inclusive of both ontology and theology as being discursive practices themselves. Whatever ontology and theology are, they are at least discursive practices and can be analyzed as such. Within the sensibilities of a postmodern incredulity toward metanarratives, I think that, before we move to frame an understanding of the symbolic in ontology, we should first examine the discourses in which symbols are imbedded and see if their characteristic functions can be understood instead as a dynamic of discursive formations.[8]

It is in textual formations and through the general tropics of discourse that the ordinary word can function extraordinarily. Various

---

8. Jean-François Lyotard, *The Postmodern Condition: A Report on Knowledge,* translated by Geoff Bennington and Brian Massumi (Minneapolis: University of Minnesota Press, 1984), p. xxiv.

figures of discourse can *turn* the discourse, *forcing* it into new patterns of meaning and significance. That is, the force of such a discourse is tropological rather than descriptive. Ontology may itself be a tropological discourse and not a metanarrative for theological subsets such as Christology or eschatology. Because of this possibility, I think that we must hesitate before the facticity of the text and interrogate the practice of theological thinking as well as its content. This is particularly important if one of the claims for a discourse is that it has a transforming power. Word as *event* is a practice.

Eschatology in general and Tillich's reflections on eschatology in particular are discourses of extreme formulations. Tillich writes that

> the Kingdom of God is also the place where there is a complete transparency of everything for the divine to shine through it. In his fulfilled Kingdom, God is everything for everything. This is a symbol of ultimate revelation and ultimate salvation in complete unity. The recognition or nonrecognition of this unity is a decisive test of the character of a theology. (ST, 1:147)

Understanding the force of this claim has far-reaching implications for understanding the character of symbolic language within theological discourse. Eschatological symbols strain what we ordinarily mean by meaning by placing severe demands on the text. "Ultimate revelation" and "ultimate salvation" are ineffable within familiar discourses. In this sense, they defamiliarize and pressure a text of ordinary meanings.

There is an interesting functional affinity between eschatological formulations within a systematic theology and the parables of Jesus. There is an obvious connection in content between eschatology and Jesus' parables of the Kingdom. But, there is more. Why did Jesus teach in parables concerning the Kingdom of God? John Dominic Crossan, in his book *The Dark Interval,* suggests the following maxim: "Parables give God room." They do this by shattering "the deep structure of our accepted world."[9] Parabolic disjunctions create

9. John Dominic Crossan, *The Dark Interval: Towards a Theology of Story* (Niles, Illinois: Argus Communications, 1975), pp. 121–22.

spaces in an ordinary discourse and thereby refigure the relationships of familiar terms.

As Crossan also points out in his book *Raid on the Articulate: Comic Eschatology in Jesus and Borges,* using the distinction of Roman Jakobson between the metaphoric and metonymic poles of language, there are metaphoric parables and metonymic parables.[10] In parables, both figurations transform the world paradoxically, but in metaphor there are associations by similarity and in metonymy there are associations by contiguity.

It is my suggestion that Tillich's eschatology functions parabolically within his theological discourse by using metonymical figurations that pressure and transform the discourse, thus refiguring ordinary relations within historical experience. The strangeness of these figurations is the making strange and incomplete the surfaces of everyday life and everyday thinking. These surfaces are experienced as the contours of finite life and, for Tillich, they are not satisfying in themselves because "the truth which does *not* disappoint dwells below the surfaces in the depth" (SF, p. 53). It is this desire for depth that in Tillich's thought justifies the deformation and transgression of the surfaces of ordinary discourse by figurations of extremity.

I am not suggesting that this is an overt strategy for Tillich but, instead, that it is a strategy implicated in his thinking both by his understanding of the symbolic function and by the actual practice of eschatological figuration within his texts. Eschatological symbols have a revolutionary character within a discourse. There is more of an apocalyptic tone than a content in Tillich's eschatology. "What is really symbolized in 'hell' and 'heaven' is the absolute seriousness of the relation to the Holy, to the Absolute itself" (MSA, p. 129). Eschatology fissures the completeness of history through judgments by placing within the transitoriness of history figurations of ultimacy and eternality.

Eternal life is equated with divine life so that eschatological figurations are one of the ways in which God is spoken of in the sym-

---

10. John Dominic Crossan, *Raid on the Articulate: Cosmic Eschatology in Jesus and Borges* (New York: Harper & Row, 1976), pp. 107–8.

bolic domain. But, this speech of God and the Kingdom of God is not speech about God but is instead a transformation of ordinary speech by pressuring it to relate to an ultimacy that it cannot contain within the rules of its own formation. Contiguous association with figurations of ultimacy can be an immanent judgment within an ongoing discourse.

In an extreme eschatological formulation, such as the ultimate judgment of the world by Christ associated with the symbol of the Second Coming, this immanent judgment makes a claim within the discourse. The inscription of the New Being within the ordinariness of thinking pressures for a decision of acceptance or rejection. The ambiguities of existence are not resolved by such a claim. Instead, within the discourse we locate a symbol of separation that negates the ordinariness of the discourse without dissolving it.

> This immanent judgment, since it is going on under the conditions of existence, is subject to the ambiguities of life and therefore demands of an ultimate separation of the ambiguous elements of reality or their purification and elevation into the transcendent unity of the Kingdom of God. (ST, 2:164)

The symbol of the Kingdom of God in Tillich's thought is peculiarly without much content. It is what it does to other discourses and to the surface of discourse that matters. Tillich talks about connotations and characteristics of the Kingdom of God which describe what is done to other discourses rather than give way to any kind of literal descriptions. He says that the Kingdom of God is political. This means that "the political symbol is transformed into a cosmic symbol, without losing its political connotation." The Kingdom of God is social. The holiness of what ought to be instantiates the unconditional moral imperative of justice. Utopian discourses are transformed by the "of God" to negate the meaning of an earthly fulfillment. The personalistic meaning of the Kingdom of God is that it gives a transhistorical aim and eternal meaning to the individual (ST, 3:358). The fourth characteristic of this symbol is its universality. All dimensions of life are implicated in this symbol (ST, 3:359). It is this implicatedness of the symbol in all dimensions of life that gives it power by a simple location within any discursive formations. Perhaps one of the clearest routes to understanding how Tillich uses the symbol of the Kingdom of God within discursive formations is to see how he compares and contrasts it with the Buddhist symbol of Nirvana. In *Christianity and the Encounter of the World Religions*, Tillich writes:

> In discussing them it becomes obvious that two different onto-logical principles lie behind the conflicting symbols, Kingdom of God and Nirvana, namely, 'participation' and 'identity.' One participates, as an individual being, in the Kingdom of God. One is identical with everything that is in Nirvana. (CWR, p. 68)

The Kingdom of God as a social, political, and personalistic symbol is contrasted with Nirvana as an ontological symbol (CWR, p. 64). What is important in this distinction is that the Kingdom of God is not an ontological symbol governed by the logic of identity, which, in the Western ontotheological tradition, would always be the determination of identity in difference. The dominant trope in a logic of identity would be metaphor. In the metaphorical copula, similarity approaches identity. The logic of differentiation is gradually effaced when the dissimilarity of elements joined in metaphorical union is overcome in the assertion of their identity. In this figuration of one-ness of identity, which is more appropriate to the symbol of Nirvana than to the symbol of the Kingdom of God, the specificities of politics, societies, and persons are not transformed or transcended but are lost in a being that is best figured as non-being.

This is not Tillich's eschatological vision. "Nothing truly real is forgotten eternally, because everything real comes from eternity and goes to eternity. . . . Nothing in the universe is unknown, nothing real is ultimately forgotten."[11] The past is transcended but not negat-

---

11. Paul Tillich, *The Eternal Now* (New York: Charles Scribner's Sons, 1956), p. 35.

ed in eternal presence. That is, in contiguous association with the eternal, the paradoxical state of the discourse is that, although everything remains the same, everything is changed. Metonymical eschatological figurations force a juxtaposition of the eternal with figures of finitude, transience, and temporality. Although the finite, transient, and temporal remain, the discursive complex in which they are inscribed has been radically transformed.

The *telos* of the discourse has been transformed by figurations of ultimacy. The discourse is denied finite closure, completion, and totalization. The unassimiliability of eschatological figurations within a finite discourse deracinates the discourse and permits a theological drift outside of the rules of its originary formation. That is, the discourse is referenced outside of itself because the rules of its formation cannot contain the association with the eschatological figure. The text is victimized by this metonymical intruder. Thus, the rather un-Tillichian notion of theological drift is simply a modest notation for the transcending of a text that is at the same time a subversion of the text.

There is a singularity about Tillich's understanding of eschatology that I think is better understood through metonymical figurations rather than metaphorical figurations, although Tillich himself uses the language of metaphor. When he talks about the meaning of the various images used to depict the "last days" or "last things," he emphasizes the singularity of the *eschaton* in preference to the plurality of *ta eschata* (ST, 3:395). He writes: "The theological problem of eschatology is not constituted by the many things which will happen but by the one 'thing' which is not a thing but which is the symbolic expression of the relation of the temporal to the eternal" (ST, 3:395). What matters is the one "thing" that pressures everything else. This one "thing" cannot be understood in the logic of identity. We are not able to discern a similarity between this one "thing" and the ordinary things of our lives. The one "thing" is an intruder into our ordinariness and our ordinary discourse.

The breaking in of the "Kingdom of God" into history and thus into discourse is, through association, an immanent and ultimate judgment. That which is negative is exposed and excluded as negative. "It is acknowledged for what it is, non-being" (ST, 3:400). Under the pressure of an eschatological figure, the negative loses it valence for eternal memory. That is, it has no associative connectedness with the dominant eschatological trope. Exclusion is a transformation within any ongoing discourse. This move is very different from the inclusiveness of metaphor, and this is why I think Tillich refers to it as the effect of negative metaphorical language (ST, 3:401).

The reference to negative metaphorical language obscures the radicality of Tillich's eschatological vision in relationship to his understanding of theological symbolism. He is not simply fashioning negative metaphors. Instead, I am suggesting that he is radicalizing discourse in an all-embracing symbolism to correspond with an instantiation of a radical negativity that is a consequence of his non-symbolic claim that God is being-itself.

We cannot say anything further about the identity between God and being-itself. In this sense, Tillich's assertion of a nonsymbolic identity is an assertion of the *otherness* of God. The symbolic language of eschatology is in a coherent relationship with the theological assertion of the identity of God with being-itself when it bears witness to the *otherness* of God. In a discussion of the history of salvation, Tillich writes: "Salvation embraces revelation, emphasizing the element of truth in the saving manifestation of the ground of being" (ST, 3:362). What is revealed is the incompleteness and inconclusiveness of history in association with the radical *otherness* of God. Ultimate judgment, the Kingdom of God, and eternal life are all symbols that metonymically intrude upon our collective and personal histories giving room for God—giving room for that which is other than the finite complex of differential signification.

The discourse is pressured by eschatological figurations into a state of epistemological and ontological undecidability. The instantiation of a negativity through eschatological symbols is not a nihilism but instead makes room for meaningful decision. This space for decision can be given voice in the language of faith or on a register of ethical decidability. What is important in this formulation is that the transforming effect of eschatology is a shift from one register of discourse to another. No discursive practice with its political, historical, and ethical implications can justify itself because eschatological figures make it incomplete by their very presence in the discourse.

This does not mean that there is a new appearance to the discourse. The shift in registers may leave the discourse looking very much like it did before the shift. What is different is the valuation and status of the concepts inscribed and formed within the discourse. Tillich's language for the transition from a temporal to an eternal register is a language of valuation. There is an exposure of the negative as negative (ST, 3:398). The *otherness* of God remains untouched by the negative while at the same time exposing the negativity of the negative within the discourse.

The universality of eschatological symbols means that all domains of experience are implicated in the space of the *otherness* of God. There is no domain of experience that is self-sufficient and a retreat from the claim of that which is other than ourselves. Tillich does not think of the end of history as a future event. He notes that "end" can mean both finish and aim (ST, 3:394). He emphasizes the existential importance of the recognition that we are "standing at every moment in face of the eternal, though in a particular mode of time" (ST, 3:395). Thus, there is no time that is self-sufficient or fulfilling in itself. The necessarily unthought *otherness* of the word "God" denies closure to any event.

This is judgment but, in Tillich's eschatology, it is also paradoxically "blessedness." "The Divine Life is the eternal conquest of the negative; this is its blessedness" (ST, 3:405). This is an ongoing process of transformation brought about by entertaining within our thinking and discourse the end of history, the *telos* of history. The transformation can be likened to a formula for transubstantiation in which the substance of the eucharistic elements are changed by a new telos, even if the matter, form, and physical forces that also constitute substance remain the same. There is a new reality in this formulation. There are new discursive realities with the metonymical presence of eschatological figurations even though there remains an awareness of unhappiness, despair, and condemnation within finite experience (ST, 3:403). The key to the force of Tillich's eschatology is the *other* in and of language. "There is no blessedness where there is no con-quest of the opposite possibility, and there is no life where there is no 'otherness'" (ST, 3:421). The all-embracing symbolism of eschatology inscribes the irre-ducible *otherness* of God into the discourse of the world. Salvation is the revelation of "the ultimate seriousness of life in the light of the eternal" (ST, 3:421). There is in this claim a depth which does not disappoint us. Eschatology is our talk of a God that remains unspo-ken and through these instantiations of negativity there is always an openness that resists the trivialization of life. The blessedness of life is a permanent critique implied in Tillich's understanding of God. The con*text* of this critique is a *text*ure that allows for nontrivial inscriptions of life's experiences.

Seven

Interventions

There is an incompleteness in Paul Tillich's systematic theology thinking. His "silent embarrassment" in speaking or writing the name of God reveals tensions and fissures on the textual surface of his thinking. The richness of his symbolic voice is always implicitly critiqued by the force of his nonsymbolic assertion identifying God with being-itself. There will always be a remainder when we shift the register of discourse from the nonsymbolic to the symbolic or if the shift is from the symbolic to the nonsymbolic. There is always an "other" of discourse. How do we access and value this "other?"

Tillich constructed a complex surface for theological thinking that would allow for deep inscriptions. He was able to do this work within the frame of the ontotheological tradition. Being maintains its primacy and mystery. The name of God maintains its mystery.

Tillich is a Christian. There is in his theology not only the "name" of God but there is also the "word" of God. This "word" is transparent language. "Something shines (more precisely, sounds) through ordinary language which is the self-manifestation of the depth of being and meaning."[1] Even more important, the "word" of God is incarnate in Jesus as the Christ. "There can be no revelation in the history of the church whose point of reference is not Jesus as the Christ" (ST, 1:132). This is a final revelation and final revelation

1. Paul Tillich, *Systematic Theology*, 3 vols. (Chicago: University of Chicago Press, 1951, 1957, 1963), 1:124. Hereafter cited in the text as ST with appropriate volume and page numbers.

84

"means the decisive, fulfilling, unsurpassable revelation, that which is the criterion of all the others" (ST, 1:133).

There is a revelatory "other" in Tillich's theology that is not immediately or obviously accessible in a secular milieu. The incompleteness of the theological surface is complemented and augmented by the uniqueness of a final revelation. Tillich understands this final revelation to have universal meaning (ST, 1:16). A problem for postmodern readers is that there is at least a nonrecognition of being a "hearer of the word." They are left with the tensions and fissures in Tillich's construction of a theological surface. Is there a different way of thinking the importance of the name of God if one is outside of the hermeneutical circle of belief?

Perhaps there is a singularity in speaking or writing the name of God. Perhaps the name of God is a paradigmatic singularity. Sometimes it cannot be spoken. Sometimes it cannot be written. As Descartes understood in his third meditation, the name of God is what subjectivity is not in its self-representation. There is an indirection or turn in theological discourse around the name of God that is an important complication in thinking about thinking. In particular, the problem of representation becomes acute when we include God in a discursive practice. Religious traditions bear witness that the name of God is always a substitution. If a Muslim can say ninety-nine names of God, the one-hundredth name is ineffable. Or, if we are Thomists and we are denied angelic knowledge, the knowledge and talk of God is analogical. These examples could be multiplied throughout the history of religions but we will always come to a representational incompleteness as an achievement of religious consciousness. Being able to think the concept of the name of God, even if that thinking includes a denial of the ability to write or speak the name of God, is a basic transcendence of subjective dominance. The subject is able to witness to its implication in what is other than its content. This is a theological exigency of mind. Thinking is able to fissure its own recording surface.

If the first phase of theological text production can be characterized as topological, the cultivation of surfaces, the second phase can be characterized as tropological. I am making the claim that theology is able to intervene in its own production, disrupt its surface, and witness to what is other than its representations. There can be expressions without representation even though they will be in the midst of representations. The meaning of this claim can be understood in relationship to the differentiation between primary and secondary processes of thinking. The question at hand is whether secondary process thinking, what we mean by consciousness in its manifestation, can in its reflectivity also reflexively cathect and effect primary process thinking. Can secondary process thinking intervene in the generative matrix from which it issues? Can secondary process thinking contribute to the privilege of its own making?

I am not making any metaphysical claims about the nature or reality of God. What is under consideration is the name of God as a discursive figure inscribed on a theological or religious surface. What does it mean to speak of the name of God in a discursive practice? What does it mean to introduce within a discursive practice a singularity that cannot be exfoliated and resists explanation? Intentionally or unintentionally, entertaining the concept of the name of God problematizes the theological surface, makes it incomplete, and puts forth the question of what else is happening in discourse. Secondary processes are unmasked as secondary processes. The name of God is a mark that suggests that there is more in discourse than representational content.

The problem of representation is not unique to theological discourse. However, in theology, the name of God makes the question of representation unavoidable. This is why I have referred to the name of God as a paradigmatic singularity. Theological discourse is pressured to turn on itself because it cannot easily stabilize its surface once it has thought the concept of the name of God. We might say that the name of God cannot be contained in the representational economy of secondary process thinking. One immediate consequence of this destabilization is that there is no advantage in eliding other singularities that have marked the discourse to maintain order since order can never be totalized. Thinking the name of God is a move against secondary processes of repression. Second, the question of a generative or primary process is valorized.

The question and problem of articulating a primary process of thinking is closely akin to the problems of thinking the unthought, saying the unsaid, or being conscious of the unconscious. The primary process will only be known as it manifests itself in the secondary process. Our strategy will have to be heuristic. We can designate a space to think about primary processes and then collect symptomatic manifestations as they mark the surfaces of ordinary experience. The space is a construct of secondary process thinking that functions as an imperative to be attentive to the vagaries of experience and distributions of singularities. It belongs to rhetoric rather than to metaphysics even when it is a metaphysical figuration. The space for thinking is a space for speaking and for writing and this speaking and writing will necessarily be experimental. We are talking about an act of engaging thinking in its own processes with the expectation that this act will be disclosive of some aspects of its internal constitution.

Primary process thinking is a materialist hypothesis. It is a positing of a world that is constituted other than its being constituted in thought and from which its constitution in thought is rendered possible. It is an affirmation that we can meaningfully think about a nexus of forces that is a matrix for thinking in the specificity of every representational economy. This does not mean that there is a single matrix that can be generalized for every representational field. Specificity suggests multiplicity without at the same time denying commonality or similarity among diverse matrices. In fact, we will have to work with commonalities in order to think the problematic of primary process thinking, but since we cannot ascertain whether these commonalities are expressions of our hypothetical perspectives or descriptive of primary processes we cannot generalize them into metaphysical principles. Their status will remain quasi-transcendental and remain implicated in the rhetoric of their manifestations.

This means that the criteria for evaluating the adequacy of both analytic and synthetic judgments will be provisional and self-authenticating within the intellectual constructs of their appearance. We will be more inclined to say yes to an intellectual construct if it carries with it the intensity of aesthetic satisfaction. This is not simply a matter of taste. Intensity is a reflexive concept that refers to the nexus of forces that we are trying to elaborate in the concept of primary process thinking. The intensity of an aesthetic satisfaction is an experience of power that is correlate with but not correspondent to representational differentiation.

There is a very definite knot in theological discourse. Thinking the concept of the name of God even when there is no name that can be spoken or written is a simple transcendence of subjective dominance, although we simultaneously recognize that thinking the concept of the name of God is within the domain of the subject. The knot is that we are always in the domain of the subject while we are seeking to bring forces to meaning that are not identical with the domain of the subject, although they are conditions of its possibility. The criteria that are used to judge the adequacy of constructions in secondary process thinking are themselves manifestations within the secondary process.

The most obvious and accessible judgment of adequacy is the judgment as to whether the diverse markings on the surface of experience are meaningfully connected. It is on this first level of judgment that singularities are particularly problematic.

Singularities disrupt the sense of connectedness. Their meaning is determined in their aftereffects and cannot always be contained within explanatory patterns. Aesthetic satisfaction in the intellectual constructions of secondary process thinking is not reducible to explanation although explanatory completeness remains an important criterion for the judgment of adequacy. But, completeness is not complete in itself. There are also intensities, pulsions, flows, and other manifestations of power or force that pressure the meaning of adequacy. Force can come to expression without representation by disturbing the representational economy in which it appears. In general, the meaning of a singularity is not its explanation but its ability to disturb, disrupt, and fissure explanatory schemes. A space opens within discourse for what is other than discourse. Meaning, which is a discursive achievement, gains significance through intensity. Significance complements meaning. However, sometimes what is a complement is itself a dangerous supplement. Meaning can give way to force.

The notion of a primary process is a construction of secondary process thinking interrogating the conditions of its own possibility. This would at first appear to be a straightforward Kantian inquiry except that with the admission of singularities into the discussion there are forces of distortion and disguise that have to be accounted for and that complicate analyses. The indeterminate markings of singularities within discursive practices seem to suggest an originary trauma and undecidability in bringing forces to textual expression that is an effect within rather than a function of secondary processes of thinking. The expression of force shows itself on the surface of discourse not as force but as a fissure, gap, knot, or distortion in the flow of the discourse. Whatever text is the present text to be analyzed, understood or experienced, it witnesses to its unique genealogy by containing undecidables among the markings of regularities and commonalities of textual production. The primary process is a Kantian problematic, but it is also a Freudian, Marxist, and Nietzschean problematic. Strategies for thinking the concept of a primary process must be complex enough to not deny secondary process thinking its variegated surfaces.

We know the surface of secondary process thinking as a differential field. On this surface, identity is in difference. When subjectivity was held to be the sole arbiter of meaning, it was possible to talk about a unity of apperception that was behind this play of differences. Constructs of primary process thinking were directed toward an understanding of an originary unity. The unity of apperception could then, through analogy, be speculatively linked to a cosmic monotheism. The name of God could be assimilated to a oneness of Being and the problem of difference would emanate from that which is One. Primary and secondary become hierarchical designations in this understanding.

There can be noted in this procedure of simulating the oneness of being a recognizable affinity with Platonism. The implications of beginning with the unity of the One are many. The play of differences in the secondary process is a play of appearances, a world of shadows. The copy is inferior to the model. The copy is valued to the degree that it is iconic, to the degree that it resembles the idea from which it is derivative. Lacking the ability to climb out of the cave of appearances, the domain of the play of differences, good thinking, philosophy, is a battle against sophistry. The Sophist lives in rhetoric, the world of simulacra, and undermines the meaning of resemblance between models and copies. Gilles Deleuze in discussing the *Sophist* says: "Plato discovers, in the flash of an instant, that the simulacrum is not simply a false copy, but that it places in question the very notions of copy and model."[2]

If we value the simulacrum, a move against Platonism, and emphasize the differential play of appearances, difference is privileged over unity and the whole notion of a primary process is redirected. This may be what Nietzsche meant by a reversal of Platonism. "So 'to reverse Platonism' means to make the simulacra rise and to affirm their rights among icons and copies. . . . The simulacrum is not a degraded copy. It harbors a positive power which denies *the original and the copy, the model and the reproduction*" (LS, p. 262).

Difference is what we experience. When Platonism is reversed, resemblance is then a product of the play of differences, an effect of simulacra. It may subsist in a domain of the possible but it has to be produced before it has any meaning. The emphasis in thinking about primary process shifts from origin to production, process, and becoming. The simulacrum is part of the machinery for production of more appearances. It is part of the mix in the productive matrix necessary for thinking and discourse. There, however, is a certain privilege to simulacra. They are the order and disorder of things that appear. They are the order and disorder of meaning. As simulacra, they are the "unfounding" of the Platonic hierarchy.

"There is no world which is not manifest in the variety of its parts, places, rivers, and the species that inhabit it" (LS, p. 266). There is a faithfulness to our experience when we begin with diversity and difference. The same, the similar, and the identical are simulations within a play of differences. We cannot step in the *same* river

2. Gilles Deleuze, *The Logic of Sense,* translated by Mark Lester with Charles Stivale (New York: Columbia University Press, 1990), p. 256. Hereafter cited in the text as LS with appropriate page numbers.

twice but we can simulate the oneness of the river and give it a name. The meaning of the *One* is a product of differential play, a simulacrum. To give it an originary meaning conflicts with the belatedness of its achievement. "Originariness" is itself a simulacrum. This is an ancient problem and we clearly are privileging Heraclitus over Parmenides, Epicurus and Lucretius over Plato and Aristotle. It is also the problem of "Modernity." As Deleuze suggests: "Modernity is defined by the power of the simulacrum" (LS, p. 265). The inability to guarantee the unity of the Cartesian subject and insure subjective dominance in the context of twentieth-century intellectual and historical experience crazed the meaning of meaning. The arts witnessed to the ability to tell several stories at the same time without a sense of an ending, to express divergent series and planes in visual representation, and to give voice to multiple tonalities. The discourses of the sciences became populated with notions of relativity, indeterminacy, and incompleteness. It is as if the nineteenth-century hermeneutics of suspicion came to meaningful expression in a return of repressed forces in and about the discourses of modernity. Consent to the significance of these discourses involves recognitions or rethinkings that resonate with the forces that came to expression.

To rethink the self as de-centered is to have a different experience of the self and the world. If we say yes to writers and artists as diverse as James Joyce, Alain Robbe-Grillet, Jorge Borges, Anselm Kiefer, and Pablo Picasso, we are saying yes because we have experienced a resonance with forces that have come to expression, although not necessarily representation, in their discourses. We say yes to these writers and artists because these forces augment our own thinking with an intensity that we value. There is a vitality in the resonance and recognition that is easily lost in the commodification of ordinary thinking. Both elements, resonance and recognition, are ingredients in the intensification of life.

Postmodern philosophy and theology is a rethinking in the wake of modernism. It is a thinking in explicit recognition of the power of the simulacrum. Its surfaces are domains of contestation because they entertain divergent series of forces released in modernist discourses and before them in the discourses of the hermeneutics of suspicion. Every definition of thinking becomes problematic because its privilege will always be contested. There is the knot. We are always in the foyer. The heuristics of thinking primary process construct a liminal space. That is, we are betwixt and between divergent series of forces and representational economies. The problem is to define a space to simulate order that does not repress diversity.

Every construct will be a problem so that strategies will have to accompany construction that turn the constructs back on their constructedness. The danger is always literalism. Simulacra become assimilated to reality. The challenge for postmodern thinking about thinking is to proceed in the development of interpretive concepts while maintaining critical principles that continue to fold the discourse reflexively.

It would seem in actual practice that many postmodern critical theorists have combined what we have earlier called metonymic strategies with metaphoric strategies to dynamically articulate primary process thinking. The primary nexus of forces have metaphorical designations such as Jacques Lacan's "the order of the nonrealized" or Julia Kristeva's "semiotic chora."[3] But, these type of metaphorical constructions are not thought of as descriptively complete. Contiguous with the metaphorical constructions are figurations of rupture, cut, and fissure that metonymically disturb the metaphorical constructions. Thinking the concept of the primary process is itself a process that includes a reflexive cathexis of the primary process that is being thought.

Descriptions of the primary process are populated with figurations that metonymically function to continually pressure the discourse toward deliteralization. Derrida's undecidables, the archetrace, *différance*, supplementarity, iterability, re-mark, hymen, and spur that function as spaces and interchangeable floating signifiers are always making way for the "other" of language by marking an other in language. Kristeva's transversal negativity intersecting the semiotic

3. Jacques Lacan, *The Four Fundamental Principles of Psychoanalysis,* translated by Alan Sheridan (New York: W. W. Norton & Co., 1978); and Julia Kristeva, *Revolution in Poetic Language,* translated by Margaret Waller (New York: Columbia University Press, 1984), pp. 117–27.

chora and the domain of the symbolic keeps drawing us toward the enigma of representational processes. With Lacan, there is a displacement of subjectivity in the accession into the symbolic, the logic of the signifier. The micropolitics of Deleuze and Guatarri contain a plethora of machinic cuts and ruptures to secure access to the forces, flows, and pulsions that constitute a dimension of the primary process. The conceptualization of the primary process is continually transgressed and destabilized in its formulation so that it represents itself as a simulacrum. We are then able to have a discourse about primary process but that discourse remains fluid and open to the process itself.

Any discourse about primary process is heuristic and provisional. To think of it as foundational is a self-admitted irony. It is better characterized as a strategic initiative in the development of a hermeneutic tropology. Since whatever figurations represent the primary process are themselves simulacra, the achievement in the development of such concepts is not that we now have principles for grounding discourse but that we have principles for turning discourse. The concept of primary process thinking is a critical notation within a play of differences that the play of differences is incomplete and not capable of completion. It is a constant pressure within discourse to convolute its surfaces, space its achievements, and perforate its figurations.

Entertaining the concept of a primary process can be a strategy from within any representational economy to complicate and mix its discursive practice with what it is not. The efficacy of the concept of a primary process is the distribution of its effects across a representational economy which is the texturing of a textual surface. For example, all representations are re-marked as simulacra. The weave of discourse is loosened. The spaces for nonrepresentational expression can be valued within a representational economy without undermining the concept of its achievement. Recognizable incompleteness can itself become valued as an achievement and an opening for intensities, a complementary significance.

We have already said that the second phase of theological text production is tropological and that the concept of primary process thinking is a strategic initiative of secondary process thinking in the development of a hermeneutic tropology. Just as we talked about the preparation of recording surfaces in the first topological phase of theological text production, the concept of primary process thinking is the preparation for strategies of intervention and transgression in the second tropological phase.

A theological tropology is, within secondary process thinking, an explicitly conscious semiotic process. It is what we do with images, words, and phrases to place them in contestation in order to loosen the differential play of signs marking the surfaces of discourse. A tropology is generated from and within the discourses of secondary process thinking. A tropology is a strategic enterprise that is intentional and thereby necessarily a secondary process. An intentionally tropological use of figurations differs from what we meant by the meaning of singularities. The singularity is an event. It can even be a word-event, a trope or figuration, that intersects a discursive practice. It is an event that is not intended within a semiotic process but that issues forth in a semiotic process. It issues forth in a series of effects marking or remarking semiotic processes. A tropology is a seeking for an access to the nexus of forces constituting the meaning of primary processes to intensify its own achievement. In contrast to the intentional trope, the singularity is an intrusion of primary processes within a discursive practice distributing its marks through the discursive practice. Tropological strategies prepare thinking for singularities.

There is no single tropological strategy for using discursive figurations to reflexively engage thinking in its primary processes. There can be analytical or synthetic procedures and mixtures of both. There can be reading or writing strategies or mixtures of both.

One of the common strategies in postmodern thinking is critique or critical intervention in already existing textual practices. Critique as intervention carries with it the awareness that "it," the text, "could always be otherwise." This thread of criticism is particularly evident when feminist critics read patriarchal texts or in the ideological or social critiques of Marxist theorists. There is an awareness that the framing of a text is political and that excluded voices mark an other that can intrude upon the text and disrupt its surfaces. Critique is a deconstruction of a textual practice even when the critic may not identify with "deconstructionist" theory. The text is read to be problematized, ruptured, fissured, opened to the excluded other.

Derrida and his deconstructionist theory are helpful for generally characterizing this tropological strategy. First, he understands the discursive status of textual production. Second, he understands the materiality of expression. Third, he is a very careful reader of texts.

It is very clear in his work that the locus of deconstruction is the given text. He is not comparing texts. He is not translating texts. He is reading texts. But, he reads in a special way. Derrida teaches us to read *in extremis*. He reads for internal tensions, inconsistencies, and constitutive complexities. He sometimes reads against the grain of the text to locate lines of fissure and expressions of absurdity. His reading technology is not unlike Freud's injunction to psychoanalysis to attend to experience with an "evenly hovering attention" noting resistances, distortions, and disproportions. These disfigurations indicate that something else is going on other than what is manifest on the surface.

A deconstructive analysis depends on the representational economy of the given text containing traces of its origination. These traces are undecidables within the text because they mark where the text is incomplete. They are an "other" within language. It is at these points and along these lines that deconstruction makes an incision emphasizing the incorrigibility of the trace to the order of the discourse. This is not an arbitrary move for Derrida. "The *incision* of deconstruction, which is not a voluntary decision or an absolute beginning, does not take place just anywhere, or in an absolute elsewhere. An incision, precisely, it can only be made according to lines of force and forces of rupture that are localizable in the discourse to be deconstructed."[4]

Deconstructive criticism is not "wild analysis," but it is a very careful reading of texts. The text is marked by its own lines of fissure and forces of disruption. What sometimes makes deconstruction

---

4. Jacques Derrida, *Positions,* translated by Alan Bass (Chicago: University of Chicago Press), p. 82.

seem esoteric and strange to ordinary language usage is that it attends to the unthought syntax of thinking. It attends to the process of representations coming into a presentational immediacy.[5] It looks for those markings within the text that witness to its genealogy.

The locus of deconstructive work is the given text but the text is not everything. In an interview with Richard Kearney, Derrida makes the claim that: "Deconstruction is always deeply concerned with the 'other' of language. I never cease to be surprised by critics who see my work as a declaration that there is nothing beyond language, that we are imprisoned in language; it is, in fact, saying the exact opposite. The critique of logocentrism is above all else the search for the 'other' and the 'other of language.'"[6] Language is a prison only when we are not engaged in some deconstructive work. Deconstructive work does not take us below or behind a text. It attends to the traces of alterity within a text. Critique engages us in primary and secondary process thinking by loosening the manifest content of a text. Thinking experiences itself as implicated in the "other" of language even if it cannot speak the name of that "other." The success and force of critique is its ability to turn discourse toward its own constitutive complexity.

Deconstructive critiques, however, are not the only strategies for loosening the weave of language. Derrida, in his more experimental and playful texts such as *Glas* or *The Postcard,* generated a writing with a loose weave by using graphic displacements, mixed genres, and difficult intertextual referencing. If we characterize the first strategy of critique as dominated by reading technologies, this second strategy could be said to be the development of writing technologies. Texts are generated that highlight their fissured surfaces, their disorder and incompleteness. The textual production can itself be likened to an erring and also to bricolage.

5. Cf. Alfred North Whitehead's discussion of presentational immediacy and causal efficacy in *Symbolism: Its Meaning and Effect* (New York: Capricorn Books, 1959), pp. 13–16.

6. Richard Kearney, *Dialogues with Contemporary Continental Thinkers* (Manchester: University of Manchester Press, 1984), p. 123.

In this second strategy there is an assembling. Inherited texts, images, and discursive figurations are conjoined or arranged on a representational surface. The linkage is metonymical. Contiguities are determined by placement and spacing so that the contiguities are contingencies. Bricolage adumbrates a fissured surface. The linkages are intersticial. There are always places to insert levers of intervention. There are spaces through which one can wander or stray. That is, bricolage generates surfaces that are amenable to an erring consciousness. The inexactness of lines of filiation give a fluidity and plurality to the assemblage of the bricoleur. With neither ground nor telos, words, images, and phrases can move about and even enter into contestation, opening spaces and continually deferring closure of the text. The work of the bricoleur is an exemplary expression and elaboration of the meaning of simulacra.

The work of the bricoleur makes things unsafe. Anything can be assimilated and/or dissimulated in text production. Established meanings can be destabilized in new assemblages. Assemblage is also dispersal and dissemination. Established meanings are sometimes affected and infected by the dissemination of meaning in new assemblages. The work of the bricoleur is a direct experiment by way of indirection within the representational process. It invokes the primary processes that it seeks to simulate.

There is a third strategy that is probably less self-conscious as a discursive strategy then deconstructive criticism or experimental writing but is a recognizable practice in much religious discourse. This is the way of parable and paradox. There is a story, a narrative, with a sense of a beginning and the expectation of an ending. The parable or paradox unexpectedly reverses the trajectory of the narrative. The turning point, the point of reversal, is an interruption, an opening, a gap, or fissure in the order of the narrative. The narrative is now unsafe. It does not insure the order of things. The turning point can be a point of intensity. It is where the text convolutes and cathects the primary process. For the hearer of the parable, the parabolic turn is a textual singularity. Force again comes to expression in the midst of representation. The force of the parable is a function of the turning point, the opening of the text. Like the work of the bricoleur, the parabler engages in a discourse that is not complete in itself. It is a mixed discourse. The significance of force supplements meaning.

There is a common feature to the various strategies that I have noted. They make a text unsafe. They all work against the effective completeness of primary repression in text production. The text can never fully transcend its genealogy and be through with the forces that move in and about its representational economy. Its material expression can be marked and remarked. There is never any guarantee of stability or singleness of purpose and the tropological strategies emphasize the unstable elements of the text. It is in this sense that, as was previously mentioned, the tropological strategies prepare thinking for singularities.

Eight

Theological Singularities: Following and Erring

I am, I exist, is necessarily true every time that I pronounce it or conceive it in my mind.

René Descartes, *The Meditations Concerning First Philosophy*

I am I because my little dog knows me.

Gertrude Stein, *The Geographical History of America or the Relation of Human Nature to the Human Mind*

There is a more significant difference between Descartes's and Gertrude Stein's articulations of the identity of the *I am* than Stein's repeatedly expressed fondness for her little dog and Descartes's absence of dog-language. The *I am* is assimilated to the *I think* in Descartes's *Meditations,* and it is the totalization of the *I think* that makes the text of the *Meditations* safe in the reconstruction of the world. For Stein, the relation of the human mind to human nature is not safe. It is subject to singularities, to intersections with the knowledge of a little dog. Intersections are interventions in the fabric of a text. They force the development of a hermeneutic tropology. That is, the subject is "in question" when it is inscribed within the tropics of discourse.

If the subject is "in question," displaced, or lost when "I am I because my little dog knows me," this is not a naive loss. What has occurred in a postmodern sensibility is a complexification of the subject that frustrates subjective dominance. Stein, Foucault, Derrida, Lyotard, or Deleuze are still able to speak or write *I,* but it is not an *I* of a transcendental unity of apperception. It is not an *I* of pure reason. It is an *I* of heterologies, empiricities, and singularities. It is an *I* that is incompatible with ontotheology.[1]

---

1. Kant defines *ontotheology* as a theology that "believes that it can know the existence of such a being [the original being] through mere concepts, without the help of any experience whatsoever" (Immanuel Kant, *Critique of Pure Reason,* translated by Norman Kemp Smith [New York: St. Martin's Press, 1965], p. 525).

This is an *I* that is known in some contemporary theological reflections and, perhaps because theologies that are not an ontotheology have learned to read experience *in extremis,* these theologies can be paradigmatic for developing strategies that can turn discourse toward its own constitutive complexity. It is the emphasis on the turns or tropes within discourse that characterizes postmodern theologies. Although singularities are events that are neither achievements nor intentions of semiotic processes, theological tropologies are explicit semiotic processes that seek no advantage by eliding singularities from the range of their interrogations. They seek to exfoliate rather than diminish life's complexities.

Robert P. Scharlemann's theology and Mark C. Taylor's a/theology are exemplary texts of a new postmodern theological thinking. Their foci and methodological strategies differ from each other. The paradigmatic singularity for Scharlemann is the instantiation of the *name* of God. The paradigmatic singularity for Taylor is the recognition of the *death* of God. Scharlemann develops deconstructive reading strategies. Taylor develops deconstructive writing strategies. These are, of course, not mutually exclusive recognitions or strategies. All of them contribute to making a text unsafe. Scharlemann seeks to think the unthought by destruing the ontotheological tradition that has allowed the otherness of God to remain unthought. Taylor seeks to think the unthought by teaching us how to say *nothing* with words.

Theology is a type of "afterthinking" for Scharlemann. It is an "afterthinking" in and of the obscurity that the world has become. In the conjunction of *I think* and *I am* the expectations of Cartesianism have been inverted so that the *I think* does not clarify the meaning of the *I am;* but, rather, "the being of things makes obscure the apparent clarity of reflection."[2]

It is not just because there are little dogs in the world that the *I*

---

2. Robert P. Scharlemann, ed., *Theology at the End of the Century: A Dialogue on the Postmodern with Thomas J. J. Altizer, Mark C. Taylor, Charles E. Winquist and Robert P. Scharlemann* (Charlottesville, VA: University Press of Virginia, 1990), p. 2. Hereafter cited in the text as TC with appropriate page numbers.

am I is obscure. There is a thickness in the presentation of the other that obscures the *I think*. "Postmodern understanding or thought involves a definite view of the obscurity of the being of the self; it involves a definite view of the connection between the end of metaphysics based on a supreme being and the meaning of the death of God; it involves a transformation of the religious "Good Friday" into a world-historical event; and, finally, it involves a definite view of replacing metaphysics of first principles with a form of thinking oriented to epochal arrangements" (TC, p. 6). This means that in postmodern theology there must be a "re-signing" of the subject.[3] The *I* is written into a new epochal arrangement of thinking and, we might say, inscribed on a newly prepared theological surface.

The preparation of this surface is a deconstructive theological task in Scharlemann's thought. The construal of *being* as presence to consciousness is an expression of subjective dominance that must be destrued if there is to be any understanding of the complex of forces and realities that constitute experience. How is this to be done? When understood within a theological domain, Scharlemann describes this work as "the task of inscribing 'God' upon all names, 'God is' upon all events, and 'God is God' upon all identities."[4] What he has recognized as properly theological is the instantiating capacity of the word "God."[5]

In his remarkable essay, "The Being of God When God Is Not Being God: Deconstructing the History of Theism," Scharlemann shows how the word "God" instantiates a radical negativity that fissures subjectivity with an otherness that is other than subjectivity.[6] This is not simply a contour on a subjective surface. It marks an open-

---

3. Robert P. Scharlemann, *The Being of God: Theology and the Experience of Truth* (New York: The Seabury Press, 1981), p. 177.

4. Ibid., p. 183.

5. Robert P. Scharlemann, *Inscriptions and Reflections: Essays in Philosophical Theology* (Charlottesville, VA: University Press of Virginia, 1989), p. 121.

6. This essay is published in both *Inscriptions and Reflections,* pp. 30–53, and in Thomas J. J. Altizer et al., *Deconstruction and Theology* (New York: Crossroad, 1982), pp. 79–108. *Deconstruction and Theology* will be cited in the text hereafter as DT with appropriate page numbers.

ing, an abyss, a gap, or fissure that resists closure and any totalization of a discursive practice.

When Scharlemann approaches the task of deconstructing the history of theism, there are obvious affinities with Heidegger's "destruction" of the history of ontology. He, however, recognizes a very important difference. The meaning of *being* may have been forgotten, covered over by metaphysical concepts, in the history of ontology. Heidegger seeks a revelation of being to redress this forgetfulness. In theology, the forgetfulness of God is a forgetfulness of the *otherness* of God (DT, p. 88). This has significant implications for what it means to think theologically in contrast with what it means to think ontologically.

Being may be what is unthought in *I am here* to beings, but being is not other to the *I am here* [*Dasein*]. Being may have to necessarily remain unthought as being-itself so that the *I am* of the *cogito* will always obscure the *I think*. Being may appear in an interrogative practice but it is not itself a singularity. And, Scharlemann notes that even in Aristotle's time it is clear that being also cannot be a generic concept since it lacks the determination necessary for a generic concept, namely, there is nothing with which it can be contrasted (DT, p. 93). Thus, Aristotle speaks of an "analogy" of being. Being is like a shadow cast throughout a discursive practice or an echo in the background of our thinking. It may be that which calls us into thinking but, in and of itself, it remains unthought. We might say that being cannot make a difference.

This claim is demonstrated in a very simple example cited by Scharlemann. The statement that "the leaf is green" and reflection upon the statement "the leaf is green" do not readily yield the meaning of the copula *is*. We cannot discern a difference between a "green leaf" and "the *being* of a green leaf" (DT, p. 100). The being of the green leaf is assimilated into the picture of the green leaf and is well contained within a discourse about green leaves. Being does not mark a fissure in our discourse. The question of being can cause us to hesitate in our thinking. We can wait for a revelation of being.

In contrast, the name of God instantiates a radical negativity within a discursive practice and is, as such, a paradigmatic singularity. "It [the word God] has the sense of 'not I' and 'not this,' the one that 'I' and 'this' are not and that is not 'I' or 'this'" (DT, p. 102). Speaking the name of God is speaking what the I is not. "[T]he word *God* refers to the otherness that is manifested upon the speaking subject or the object spoken of or both" (DT, p. 102). Discourse convolutes and fissures its surface when it speaks the name of God because it cannot contain the meaning of that which we "cannot think" of as greater than our capacity to "think."

Speaking or writing the name of God is a singularity that functions as a deconstructive lever in the preparation of a surface for theological inscription. The surface of the text has itself been made unsafe. It is uneven and fissured wherever the words "God," "God is," or "God is God" have been inscribed. The name of God is an inassimilable trope within any discursive practice if we simply attend to the "being of God when God is not being God."

The variegation of the inscriptive surface is a primary phase in Scharlemann's theological text production. The surface has been prepared for thinking, speaking, and writing the *I am* in new arrangements that acknowledge and seek to recognize the complexity of the other in and of the self. The surface of the text has been prepared to constantly challenge and interrogate subjective dominance. The possibility is opened to experience the "I am I because my little dog knows me."

If we characterize the first phase of Scharlemann's theological text production as tropological, we can characterize a second phase as topological and typological. He marks the *topoi* as indicated by ways of speaking that manifest the self.[7] These markings adumbrate a basic typology of possibilities for the construction of the self. These are structural possibilities that are actualized only in the singularities of experience. However, the opening of these possibilities encourages a more acute observation of the complex actualities of experience and, of course, thinking possibility is an act and actuality in itself.

---

7. Robert P. Scharlemann, *The Reason of Following: Christology and the Exstatic I* (Chicago: University of Chicago Press, 1991), p. 139. Hereafter cited in the text as RF with appropriate page numbers.

The affirmation of the self as a thinking being in the argument of the *cogito* is, first of all, a valuation of the incorrigibility of mind that is self-authenticating. "The modern I is, thus, the I that appears as a phenomenon in the midst of the impossibility of its being eradicated by the activity of its own thinking" (RF, p. 5). This I can be abstracted as a universal singular, but its appearance even in Descartes's argument is the appearance of an *I am here*. *I am here* in my dressing gown in front of the fire in acts of meditation.

The actuality of the *I am here* does not eradicate the possibility that I could be elsewhere, that I am also elsewhere. I am able to think this possibility even if it is not actual. The *cogito* instantiates the I but has no purchase on containing the I. Certainly the self can think the possibility of being outside of itself in its simple location. Once this possibility is thought, what remains to be thought are the criteria by which such a thought makes a credible claim within the representational economy of self-assertion. What appears in the instantiation of an ecstatic I that does not appear in the I of pure actuality engendered in methodical doubt?

Scharlemann complicates the appearance of the I by a formal analysis of possible modes of thinking that discloses the contingency of singular events which are woven into these modes of thinking and which, in turn, constitute the being-there of the self. He asserts that "[t]hinking is the openness of the self to what is other than thinking and reason is the configuration of this openness" (RF, p. 62). The openness to what is other than thinking puts the self at risk while at the same time it makes the self accessible for what can be given from what is other than the formality of thinking.

First, the self can experience a form of doubt that is not methodological but might better be described as existential. This is a doubt that leads not to certainty but to uncertainty. This is the doubt that is experienced in the disclosure of "the uncommon singularity of the I in the attack of conscience" (RF, p. 7). This is the doubt of Luther rather than Descartes. "In Luther, the subject overtaken by doubt is accused and condemned by the attacker. In Descartes, the subject undertaking to doubt assures itself of itself" (RF, p. 8).

The attacker, conscience, reveals an I that is an I of the *I am not*.

The I appears in an obligation that is inscribed as the discrepancy between *I am* and *I am not*. The relationship to the *not* is a possibility for a *can be*. It is then the combination of *not* and *should* in the voice of conscience that makes us uncomfortable in our being-in-the-world. Scharlemann refers to Heidegger, who thinks of conscience as "the call of care from the uncanniness of being-in-the-world" (RF, p. 17).

The relationship to the *not* initiates an exchange. Something is given in the call of conscience. Something is given that I am not. The *I am not* marks the negative possibility of the self. In its most extreme formulation the relation to the *I am not* is death. "[D]eath is the possibility of having no possibility of being in the world" (RF, p. 20). The I appears as finally answerable to the *not*.

But, this is not the same as saying that death is an answer to life. Death appears in the form of pure possibility. It is "a genuine 'I can' that can never become an 'I do' or 'I did'" (RF, p. 19). It is a metonym within a representational economy of self-assertion constantly pressuring the ecstasis of self. Since we cannot finally escape the ecstasis of the self, the question is, how are we going to live it. There is something other than self-assertion and self-determination, and the appearance of the *I am not* does not exhaust the possibilities for an ecstasis of the self.

In a second explication of the ecstatic self, Scharlemann takes as a guide the ethics of the theologian Wilhelm Herrmann. He asks Herrmann's question, "How [can there] be an ethos other than an ethos of self-assertion, for self-assertion is the natural drive in things?" (RF, p. 20). Can something happen that breaks into the circle of self-assertion? Herrmann says yes. "This something is an event and an appropriation. The event takes place when it *happens* that someone we meet fills us with 'respect' and 'trust'" (RF, p. 21). This meeting, if it *happens*, frees us from the "unlimited power of natural life."

The I of trust appears as an I in its freedom. By showing what we can be, the *I can be* is convertible into the appearance of the I of *I can do*. This transition is clearly distinguishable from the ultimate limit placed on a relation to death as the doing of the *I cannot*.

There is a third possibility for understanding the ecstatic self that is central to Scharlemann's theology, the I who follows. The structural problem and need for the "I am" of following is that "[i]n the normal relations, I never come into view at all within the world, since I am the perspectival center from which everything is thought, sensed, done, acted upon and to which all appears . . . I am one step removed from all that appears" (RF, p. 50).

In discussing Jesus' call to follow me, Scharlemann writes, "[o]n the face of it, this is a call to the self to come to its own, to be 'I,' in the midst of being in the world by dwelling in a message of peace. The *Unheimlichkeit* of Dasein is its peace. The self is summoned to be wholly itself in the message that is borne" (RF, p. 30). The call is a call to become what one already is. The disciples lose themselves and their worldly cares in the I am of Jesus and thus find themselves, the I am, in the I am of Jesus. The I am of the self is mirrored in the I am that calls to follow. The acoluthetic summons overcomes the perspectival rift from all that appears. "If there were no Christ-figure in the world, the 'I' of the here-and-now would be a point of view from which everything is viewed and understood but could not itself be seen and understood" (RF, pp. 157–58).

Scharlemann names the I of the I who follows an exstantial I. "The exstantial I is exterior, its summons comes from without, and yet it is identical with one's interiority" (RF, p. 139). But, this is not thought of as a narcissistic relation because the encounter with the I am is the encounter with a real figure, a person different from my own (RF, pp. 144–45).

The key to understanding the possibility for the exstantial I is that there is a reason of following, acoluthetic reason. A claim is made that, alongside of "pure" reason, the reason of conscience, and ethical reason, there is acoluthetic reason. This entails the implication "that subjectivity in one person is capable of encountering not only an analogy of its own inwardness in the person of the other, but also the identity of its own I in the other" (RF, p. 147).

The reason of following is understood to be an essential possibility of selfhood and is not restricted to exemplification in Christianity. However, in Scharlemann's theology, I think it is fair to say that the Christ-event is a paradigmatic representation of acoluthetic reason. In Christianity the authority of the Christ-figure is that the *exousia* or "being out" of the Christ and the ecstasis of the one coincide. "If Jesus was the Christ for his disciples, and if he is the Christ for followers today, then his person so affected and affects them that they recognize in him their own being" (RF, p. 117). The immediate problem for thinking the *exousia* of the Christ-figure today is its embodiment and presence as other. This is first a general problem for the appearance of the I in any of its modalities. Scharlemann affirms that what is common is that language is the material of appearance. "The I that is hidden in the anonymity of the general subject is one that appears in the use of everyday language. The exstantial I is the I which appears in the language which summons to following and also in the donative language that expresses the giving of the self to another and which comes to itself in giving itself away" (RF, p. 102).

Scharlemann also notes that the notion of textuality gives an autonomy to language so that language is a material medium and not simply a tool or convenience of thinking. "The textuality of texts is their quality of being there in the world as intelligible entities" (RF, p. 183). Writing is a material meaning that can be with us, other than us, and "a living voice of the exstantial 'I am'" (RF, p. 187). The text is a material condition that makes possible a continuation of the meaning of dwelling with the other even when the original configuration of the other has passed. We can dwell in the world and we can dwell in the word. The word can be spoken and it can be written. "To dwell in the world is to exist in such a way that one understands oneself by reference to the cares that are laid upon one by the world itself . . . dwelling in the word means to understand oneself by reference to the meaning contained in the sayings" (RF, p. 161). Scharlemann affirms that dwelling in the word is an appropriation of the resurrection presented as a gift from the exstantial I. "Knowing the truth means being in that mode of existence in which one as an authentic I both is answerable for having to die and is recipient of the gift of being beyond death" (RF, p. 162).

The ecstatic I is always the singularity of a gift. There is the gift of possibility in the *not* in conscience. There is the gift of possibility in trust and friendship. There is the gift of being beyond death in the external and exstantial I.

To what extent are these gifts dependent upon particular modes of dwelling? How does one gain access to the communal or textual bodies in which the words of conscience, friendship, or the summons to follow are spoken? It is never simply a matter of reflection or mirroring. An intersection is required, an intersection with death, a friend of respect and trust, or the Christ-figure.

The articulation of acoluthetic reason is the articulation of a promise that is also a threat. There are shadows to Scharlemann's theology that also need to be explored. The promise is clear. We can live authentically in the word, which is how we can live authentically in the world. The shadows are more complex.

On the simplest level there is a threat of exclusion. If acoluthetic reason is the possibility for authentic life, to either not hear or to not follow the call to follow is to be excluded from the satisfaction or fulfillment of authentic life.[8] The I that is denied ecstatic fulfillment appears empty or impoverished and situated in a nihilistic world. The path to authentic existence depends on the singularity of a moment of grace. Without grace there is the terrible *no* of neo-orthodox theology to the ordinariness of the world.

It appears to me that Scharlemann's move against exclusion through circumstance is the availability of the textual embodiment of acoluthetic reason. Christians can dwell in the written sayings of Jesus and their exfoliation in scripture, theology, and preaching. His appeal is to the power and singularity of a word-event.

This is a move back to the Bible that might be problematic for his secular readers. There can be cultural or social distances that veil what must be a self-authenticating power of the witness to the exstantial I. There are also problems of textuality itself that may resist Scharlemann's understanding of an inscribed witness.

8. This claim is comparable to Tillich's claim that the promise of ultimate fulfillment which is accepted in the act of faith is accompanied by a threat of exclusion from that fulfillment if the unconditional demand of faith is not obeyed. See Paul Tillich, *Dynamics of Faith* (New York: Harper & Row, 1958), p. 2.

The coming to representation in a discursive practice is a process that involves complex tropes of substitution, displacement, and condensation in a differential play. The problems of perspectivalism are more akin to accounting for the traces of Derrida's *différance* or Freud's primary repression than to an accounting for differences in location. Following a Kantian wound that is further complexified by the hermeneutics of suspicion, the perspectival problem that "I never come into view at all within the world" is not subject to resolution. The genealogy for the inscription of the I within a tropics of discourse is a riddle of specificities. It is hard to understand what it means to say that the other in a relation "is identical with the I of the self and is recognized as such" (RF, p. 117).

The claim that the call is a call to become what one already is appears at least on the surface demonstrably false. I am my specific history. "I am I because my little dog knows me." There is no congruence between the I am of Jesus of Nazareth, the I am of the textual Jesus of the Gospels, and the I am of the specific vicissitudes of my history. It is likely that my little dog does not know Jesus. Even if it is granted that the *exousia* of the Christ and the ecstasis of the one coincide, this does not mean that what one already is coincides with the ecstasis of the one. Something is lost in this possible noncoincidence even if something is gained. The measure and value of this loss and gain is important in the measure and value of our lives.

What is lost may not simply be an idiosyncratic genealogy indexed in the theater of personal memory and marked in the inscription of one's own name. It appears that Scharlemann privileges acoluthetic reason even as it is placed beside theoretical, practical, and aesthetic reason. It is inevitable that it be privileged if it is the condition for an authentic journey to selfhood. What is not inevitable but is always a risk is that the discourses of acoluthetic reason will hegemonically displace other discourses of respect, trust, and ordinary love.

If we return to Herrmann's question as to whether anything can happen to break into the circle of self-assertion, we see a valuation of the difference of the other that appears to be lost in acoluthetic reason. The other of ethics, friendship, and love is not identical with

one's interiority. There is an experience of outwardness and difference rather than inwardness and identity.

The other is not an abstract concept of "otherness" that can be
assimilated into my own subjectivity. The other is what I am not. The
other is thick with specificity that is not me. There is a distance but
not an infinite distance between the other and me. The other is not
a radical instantiation of negativity. The other is not the name of God
but she or he has a name. It is important not to subordinate that
name to the generality of possibility. Love, whether it be in friendship or romance, also gives expression to the donative power of language.

It is the intensity of love that is generalized and thereby dimly
figured in so much theological thinking. To love the other is to experience a rift, a partition in the being of the I am I. There is a nonidentity that may be more important than identity in the filling-full
of life. Jean-Luc Nancy, in an essay on "Shattered Love," makes a
claim that theology cannot ignore in its discourses of fulfillment.
"Love does not transfigure finitude, and it does not carry out its transubstantiation in infinity . . . Love cuts across finitude, always from
the other to the other, which never returns to the same—and all
loves, so humbly alike, are superbly singular. Love offers finitude in
its truth; it is finitude's dazzling presentation."[9] This is not a disclosure of meaning that should be theologically subordinated. There is
always a risk that finitude's dazzling presentation could be lost in the
discourse of the infinite. This is a risk and not a necessary implication
of Scharlemann's account of acoluthetic reason.

What is a necessary implication of Scharlemann's account of acoluthetic reason and generally of the ecstatic I is the absolute contingency of events that actualize these possibilities. The ecstatic I always
requires a gift, but there is no guarantee of a giver.

If "I am I because my little dog knows me," there is no guarantee that there will be a little dog that knows me. This is an affirma-

9. Jean-Luc Nancy, *The Inoperative Community,* translated by Peter Conoer, Lisa
Garbus, Michael Holland, and Simona Sawhney (Minneapolis: University of Minnesota Press, 1991), p. 99.

tion that I can make only after the fact of the experience. The gift of the *not* is not itself contingent, but it is a terror of ecstasis that suspends the I am I as it awaits a contingent further calling or gift. It is a terror that may not be resolved. The I am I of friendship and love, respect, and trust is wholly contingent. It is a chance meeting. It doesn't always happen. If it happens, it is wonderful.

The exstantial I and acoluthetic reason are more problematic. Scharlemann is both imaginative and correct in asserting the possibility of acoluthetic reason. But the actualization of the exstantial I is more than the assertion of a possibility. There must be, in fact, historically and then textually, an I am that is also a call to follow. This must be an I am that is coincident with the I am that I am in my ecstasis. An affirmation must be made that is more than noting an exigency of reflexive thinking. A witness is borne within the discourse of Scharlemann's theology. "To know the truth is to come into one's own in the double sense of appropriating one's own having to end and of appropriating the resurrection as a gift from the external or exstantial I" (RF, p. 162). A witness is borne to the resurrection as a gift.

Scharlemann has carried Christian witness into a postmodern sensibility. There is nothing easy, intellectually or religiously, about his thinking. He does not prescind from the implications of what he understands to be the promise, risk, and threat of affirming the possibility of acoluthetic reason. What is finally at stake in actualizing the I am of the exstantial I is that a call to follow has occurred and that I say yes to the call. The affirmation of acoluthetic reason is a promise and not a threat only when there is an accompanying affirmation of the contingent necessity of the incarnation. What is necessary for an authentic actualization of acoluthetic reason is the free, contingent expression of God's love. Scharlemann's theology requires the witness that "God so loved the world, that he gave his only Son. . . ." Without the incarnation, the word "God" is the instantiation of a radical negativity. With the incarnation, the word "God" is a gift of authentic self-recognition inscribed in the texts of the Gospel narratives.

The question of the incarnation means that everything is in question. Scharlemann knows that "[a] theological symbol within acolu-thetic reason . . . must allow for both a critical, rejecting relation to itself (the 'No' of those who do not follow) and also an affirmative, accepting relation (the 'Yes' of the follower)" (RF, p. 200). However, the singularity of the gift of the "follow me" may not seem credible. The voice of Jesus is not the only voice of the "other" in a pluralistic world. The proclamation of Jesus is always set alongside other proclamations that can also make a claim on their hearer.

Nietzsche's madman, after proclaiming the death of God, said: "I have come too early . . . my time is not yet. This tremendous event is still on its way, still wandering, it has not yet reached the ears of men."[10] This too is a singularity.

At the end of the twentieth century, this event may still be wandering, erring, pressuring, and marking the texts of literature, philosophy, and theology. It is an event within secular culture that questions and challenges the christological "follow me." Here we turn to Mark Taylor as Mark Taylor has attended not to the singularity of the name of God or to the singularity of the Christ-event but rather to the singularity of the death of God. How is this claim further articulated? How is the singularity of the death of God exfoliated? Taylor has written: "it would not be too much to suggest that *deconstruction is the 'hermeneutic' of the death of God.*"[11] If this is a credible claim, we might want to further suggest and then interrogate the claim that the theology of the death of God is fully implicated in a postmodern sensibility and that the postmodern sensibility is fully implicated in the theology of the death of God. Perhaps a theology of the death of God gives a better clue to the sensibilities of postmodern thinking than Scharlemann's reason of following. Perhaps the movements within postmodern culture resonate more profoundly with erring rather than following.

Taylor and Scharlemann draw from much of the same philo-

10. Friedrich Nietzsche, *The Gay Science,* translated by Walter Kaufmann (New York: Vintage Books, 1974), p. 2.

11. Mark Taylor, *Erring: A Postmodern A/theology.* (Chicago: University of Chicago Press, 1984), p. 6. Hereafter cited in the text as EPA with appropriate page numbers.

sophical work in articulating their theological visions. Both question the ontotheological tradition. It is clearly the writings of Jacques Derrida and Martin Heidegger that first pressured theology to contemplate its end as a correlate to the end of philosophy and the collapse of the ontotheological tradition. Heidegger had long been associated with theological thinking in the twentieth century, but Derrida was not part of the theological conversation in any important way until the publication of Carl Raschke's *The Alchemy of the Word: Language and the End of Theology* in 1979, *Deconstruction & Theology* by T. J. J. Altizer et al. in 1982, followed by Taylor's very influential *Erring: A Postmodern A/theology* published in 1984. Since then there has been a plethora of books and articles discussing and evaluating the relationship between deconstruction and theology. The questions that are persistently asked are: (1) Is theology possible at the end of the twentieth century? and (2) If it is possible, is it meaningful? Taylor has more of an affinity with Derrida and Scharlemann has more of an affinity with Heidegger.

Taylor set the agenda for much of this theological discussion with his programmatic interrogation of the challenges to theological thinking in Part I of *Erring*. Part I is subtitled "Deconstructing Theology," and it is here that he argues for an intricate relationship between God, self, history, and book that is then followed by analyses of the death of God, the disappearance of the self, the end of history, and the closure of the book.

The metaphorics of transgression that Taylor seeks to articulate are not simple negations. He is not simply putting a minus sign in front of a term to create a dyadic opposition. Reversal and "inversion, in other words, must simultaneously be a perversion that is subversive. . . . What is needed is a critical lever with which the entire inherited order can be creatively disorganized. It is at this point that deconstruction becomes a potential resource for the a/theologian" (EPA, p. 10).

Taylor established his reputation with scholarly studies of Hegel and Kierkegaard before the publication of *Erring,* and he is profoundly aware that writing is never fully original but is always secondary and derivative. Thus, one meaning of to err is to ramble, to stray, and to wander in and through the inherited textual tradition seeking gaps or fissures into which the reader can insert levers of intervention to resist the movement of the text toward closure and completeness. Rather than an abandonment of tradition, Taylor's deconstructive a/theology is a *strong* reading of the tradition. *Erring* has a deep resonance with Rodolphe Gasché's claim that: "The deconstructive undoing of the *greatest totality,* the totality of onto-theology, faithfully repeats this totality in *its* totality while simultaneously making it tremble, making it *insecure* in its most assured evidences."[12]

In *Erring,* Taylor traces the death of God primarily in its modern humanistic expression. It is a combination of Luther's Reformation insistence on a personal relationship with God and Descartes's decisive turn to the subject, thereby implicating theology in anthropology, that culminates in a need for the death of God to liberate the humanistic subject. What Taylor notes and what drives reflection into a postmodern sensibility is that "the death of God is at the same time the death of the self" (EPA, p. 20). He says that there are two readings of death and, "Within the 'theological' register, the difference between apocalypse and disaster is the difference between two readings of the death of God" (TC, pp. 49–50). Disaster is an endless deferral of presence.

What is lost with the death of God is a fixed meaning of presence that grounds identity in difference. "In the ontotheological tradition of the West, God is virtually indistinguishable from the power of Being or Being-itself" (EPA, p. 36). Whether it is Thomas Aquinas's formulation of God as *actus purus* or Paul Tillich's claim that the only nonsymbolic theological statement about god is that "God is being-itself," the tradition has construed God as the permanent substratum of things including the identity of the self.[13]

Taylor, like Scharlemann, examines the constitution of the *I am*

12. Rodolphe Gasché, *The Tain of the Mirror: Derrida and the Philosophy of Reflection* (Cambridge: Harvard University Press, 1986), p. 180.
13. Paul Tillich, *Systematic Theology* (Chicago: University of Chicago Press, 1951), vol. 1, pp. 185, 238.

and he also first turns to Descartes. Again, the constituting of the self as subjectivity, an achievement of Cartesianism, privileges what is present to consciousness as the meaning of reality. But, this construction of the self is not its own ground. Just as the *I am* is grounded in the *I think*, the *I think* is implicated in the *I am*. "The *I am*, being experienced as an *I am present*, itself presupposes the relationship with presence in general, with being as presence."[14] That is, the *I think* means *I am present*, for which a notion of presence is a condition of its possibility. The death of God as a deferral of presence unmoors the certainty of the *cogito*. The self that first appeared to be able to stand over against God in a humanistic liberation now appears to have been implicated in the meaning of God as its own condition when inscribed within the ontotheological tradition. Both self and God are eclipsed with the deconstruction of the ontotheological tradition. The death of God and the disappearance of the self are both metaphorical expressions of the deferral of presence.

Taylor extends his deconstructive analyses to the concepts of history and the book. What he notes is that both of these concepts carry with them shadows of *logocentrism* and that they are theological notions. He quotes from H. R. Niebuhr: "To be a self is to have a God, to have a God is to have a history, that is, events connected in a meaningful pattern; to have one God is to have one history."[15] There is one master narrative. There is one book of encyclopedic proportions.

What is intriguing in Taylor's analyses is that he sees that the death of God proclaimed by Nietzsche follows the proclamation of *absolute knowledge* by Hegel. It is Hegel's proclamation of absolute knowledge that is both the end of history and the closure of the book. "Since absolute self-presence in consciousness is the infinite *vocation* of full presence, the achievement of absolute knowledge is

---

14. Jacques Derrida, *Speech and Phenomena and Other Essays on Husserl's Theory of Signs,* translated by David Allison (Evanston: Northwestern University Press, 1973), p. 54. Hereafter cited in the text as SP with appropriate page numbers.
15. H. Richard Niebuhr, *The Meaning of Revelation* (New York: Macmillan, 1967), p. 59.

the end of the infinite, which could only be the unity of the concept, logos, and consciousness in a voice without *différance*" (SP, p. 102). Absolute knowledge is total presence. There is nowhere to go. The notion of meaningful history has come to an end and Hegel is the last philosopher of the book (EPA, 76). Logocentric full presence forms an ordered totality. "This omnipresent logos is the foundation that structures the systematic theologian's book . . . Like the novelist who can no longer finish novels, the painter who cannot frame pictures, and the composer who hears no harmony, the theologian who realizes the implications of the closure of the book must become a 'writer'" (EPA, p. 79).

What does it mean to write after the end of history? Time clearly continues and books clearly have been written after Hegel. If history ends in a deferral rather than in apocalypse, and if the book comes to closure but not completeness, we see the implicatedness of these events in the disappearances of the Author of the Book and subsequently of the author of the book (EPA, pp. 80–82). There is no proper book and the book is no longer property. The gathering of meaning is a dispersal.

Taylor is not faulting Hegel as an inadequate thinker. It is precisely because Hegel is the consummate thinker of logocentrism that, when history ends but time continues and the book is closed but never complete, Western thought begins to drift and its center is displaced. It is because the consummate expression of the ontotheological tradition is not seamless that it can be the host for parasitic suspicion. As Taylor suggests, the closure of the book is the opening of the text (EPA, p. 93).

In Part II of *Erring*, "Deconstructive A/theology," the challenge to Taylor is to develop strategies for the writing of God and to assess the implications of these strategies for self, history, and text. His understanding of writing generally follows the contours of Derrida's critique of the transcendental signified and privileges Derrida's understanding of *différance* and all of its substitute expressions. "[T]he signified is a signifier. Consciousness, therefore, deals *only* with signs and never reaches the thing itself. More precisely, the thing itself is not an independent entity [be it 'real' or 'ideal'] to which all signs refer but is itself a *sign*" (EPA, p. 105). A/theological writing is a free signifying play. In what would be a surprising move to nontheological readers, Taylor claims that a/theology is radically christological. "Radical christology is *thoroughly* incarnational—the divine '*is*' the incarnate word" (EPA, p. 103). The word is embodied such that "the God of writing is manifested as the writing of God" (EPA, p. 116). This is a dissemination and not an expression of acoluthetic reason since 'writing is 'founded' by the differences it 'founds'" (EPA, p. 119). We are immediately confronted with a paradox of a nonoriginal origin. "In other words, writing is always in other words" (EPA, p. 119). Because of the inability to return to the father, the inability to grasp the transcendental signified, "the dissemination of the word replaces sterile stability and univocacy with creative instability and equivocacy" (EPA, p. 120).

The writing strategies delineated by Taylor have already been likened to a metaphorics of transgression. The text is victim. The radical *kenosis* of incarnation is the embodying of the transcendent word that is also an imbedding of the word in a signifying play so that there can be no claim to transcendence or to the transcendental signified. Because this writing has a nonoriginal origin, there is no trace of transcendence but only the trace of *différance* as the origin of differences. A/theological writing is a writing of resistance marking fault lines throughout the totalizing projects of the ontotheological tradition.

The destabilization of the "repressive logic of identity" in the signifying play of a/theological writing, in the dissemination of meaning, has important consequences for self, history, and text. Being given a proper name, self-proximity and self-presence no longer have simple meanings. "If language is not subjected to the logic of exclusion but is interpreted as a ceaseless play of interrelated differences, then the subject is both *desubstantialized* and *deindividualized*" (EPA, p. 135). It is not the self that is lost, but it is the proper self, pure subjectivity, clean and well-lit, that is stained and wound-ed by the retention of difference from its nonoriginal origin. The self does not disappear. What is dissolved are its clean and proper boundaries. The self is dispersed. The self is an affair of the other. The writing of God as a dissemination of meaning and the dispersal of the self mock a teleological notion of history. To err, to wander, to drift are behaviors more fitting the life of carnival than the pronouncements of a holy history. There is no sublation of the ordinary into a teleological whole or onto a universal plane of meaning. There is no coming to an end. The carnival is in the middle of life. There is a delight in the surface of appearances. "Festive play is an unending game in which the extraordinary becomes ordinary and the ordinary becomes extraordinary. The realization of this coincidence of opposites spreads the incarnate word and extends the divine milieu" (EPA, p. 169). A/theology inscribes a divine ordinariness.

This productivity is possible because, with the closure of the book, the text is radically open. Without a grounding logos, signifiers float within a nomadic economy of meaning (EPA, p. 175). A/theology does not wait expectantly for a secret meaning, a saving *gnosis*. Texts are contexts, although they do not exhaust the meaning of context. They stand in a "tangled relationship of coimplication" (EPA, p. 179). Texts are a making, a weaving, a stitching together. Taylor likens the a/theologian to a tailor. "The tailor, after all, is profoundly interested in surfaces and completely preoccupied with appearances. His task is to cover rather than strip, to veil instead of unveil. Above all the tailor realizes that surfaces are not superficial" (EPA, p. 180). To realize that surfaces are not superficial and that interpretation does not come to closure are promises of an a/theology. The end of the sense of the end is not a nihilism but is instead a celebration, a complexification, a carnival.

The celebrative, the complex, and the carnivalesque all have to do with what is other than the self construed as pure subjectivity. There is movement toward alterity that in a "tangled web of associations" can become "altarity."[16] Edith Wyschograd, in a review essay of *Altarity*, says that "*Altarity* is a praxis, a text, an outwork but it is

16. Mark Taylor, *Altarity* (Chicago: University of Chicago Press, 1987), p. xxix.

not a book."[17] Unlike *Erring*, but indebted to it, the dominant trope in the strategic unfolding of *Altarity* appears to be metonymic rather than metaphoric. This is a strange claim because at first *Altarity* appears to be a sophisticated introduction and presentation of primarily philosophical studies that are representative of both the background and foreground of deconstructive hermeneutics in literary theory, philosophy, and theology. In this sense it is an important theoretical companion to his anthology *Deconstruction in Context: Literature and Philosophy*. Taylor is teaching the reader how to read.

However, the significance of the book is twofold and it is only when we recognize its double agenda that we can see its continuity with the celebration of the carnival in *Erring*. First, it is an important historical study of sources introducing the lesser-known precursor figures Georges Bataille, Maurice Blanchot, and Emmanuel Levinas; it is an important and complex reading of G. W. F Hegel and Søren Kierkegaard; and it provides an elucidating analysis of difficult modern and postmodern figures such as Martin Heidegger, Jacques Lacan, Julia Kristeva, and Jacques Derrida.

I would agree with Wyschograd that, as intellectual history, "*Altarity* is, by far, the most sophisticated and perceptive account to date of a 'movement' comprising literary and philosophical tendencies that attempt to expose the presuppositions and dissimulations of Western philosophy's understanding of being, time, and language" (EW, p. 115). For example, the analysis of Derrida's *Glas* is exemplary of the quality of Taylor's intellectual historical analyses as he introduces and moves the discussion of deconstruction toward an increasingly complex weave of philosophical concepts. Throughout the book, Taylor locates the importance of Hegel for the contemporary discussion of deconstruction and gives a deep reading of the Hegelian problematic in Heidegger, Maurice Merleau-Ponty, and other precursors and players of postmodern philosophical discourses. These are but a few suggestions of how Taylor makes an important

---

17. Edith Wyschograd, "Theology in the Wake of the Other," *Journal of the American Academy of Religion* 56 (no. 1): 115. Hereafter cited in the text as EW with appropriate page numbers.

contribution to historical scholarship because of his abilities to do strong readings of difficult texts.

Within the development of his work as an intellectual historian Taylor is also recovering and sometimes nuancing important concepts that will pressure critical deconstructionist literature. However, what is more important, or at least more exciting, is that Taylor is again marking out his own philosophical and theological position. Taylor writes with a double agenda.

The originality of his book is that it is a practice of philosophical and theological thinking that works against the text as a book in the ordinary sense of what we mean by a book. Not only is the text fissured by reproductions of visual works of art and drawn into the marginalia of Kierkegaardian doodles, but Taylor also reiterates that Hegel is the last philosopher of the book and understands that he [Taylor] must be a philosopher of writing. Akin to Derrida, he writes with two hands at the same time. With one hand he elucidates an intellectual, historical context and with the other he fashions a new text. This is particularly evident in his deconstructive reading of Kierkegaard that is then doubled by a Kierkegaardian reading of the deconstructive movement.

His close attention to language and style is part of the strength of the book, but it is also part of the difficulty of the book. What he is doing with what he is saying is as important to understanding this book as what he is saying.

The "otherness" of language is written into his study of the "otherness of language." The text is descriptive and performative and its importance resides in both functions. It is a teaching book and a thinking book and ironically it is both because he writes against it being a book. He forces a juxtaposition of ideas, images, and persons, thus metonymically destabilizing the meaning of a book. The reader becomes increasingly aware of not what is thought but of what is unthought in this work. Wordplays, etymologies, and intertextual references put the unthought in expectation of the not-yet-been-thought. The danger to his project is that this could be an extension and a privileging of language and not a confrontation with the otherness of language.

Taylor is not unaware of this danger. He says that the framework of his analyses is the "unheard-of" thought of *altarity*. The question that is left in the wake of *Erring* and *Altarity* is: If the a/theologian must become a writer, how does he or she write the unheard-of thought of altarity? This question multiplies into a series of questions in Taylor's 1990 publications. To err, to stray, to wander become explicitly complemented by *to wonder*. Questions—of what is? what if? how to? how can?—populate these essays. Without an absolute origin, without a ground and without a telos, there is a coincidence of wandering and wondering.

"The task of thinking at the end of theology is to think beyond the end of theology by thinking the 'beyond' of an end that is not theological. . . . But what has theology not thought?"[18] What is clear in these essays is that for Taylor the radical experiment with thinking the unheard-of thought of altarity is not to think the *being* of others or the other. "In thinking the being of beings, ontotheology leaves nothing unthought . . . ontotheology leaves nothing unthought by not thinking nothing" (TR, p. 204). The task for a/theology is to think *nothing*. The question is: "How to do Nothing with Words" (TR, pp. 203–31). The strategy remains transgressive. He uses language against language (TR, p. 108). "What if an essay were nothing . . . nothing but a title? What if a work were . . . nothing but frame(s)?" (TC, p. 43). To think the title, to think the frame, to think the edge is to think unendingly—nothing ending nothing.

Taylor's a/theology is conceived of as a deferral of meaning. It is not as if this were a simple choice. Radical philosophical and theological thinking ironically deracinates the privilege of the subject. Deconstructive thinking is surprisingly empirical. Presence is experienced as absence and identity is experienced in difference. There is no immediate experience of a primary reality from which other realities can be derived. The construal of being as presence is a reality mediated by processes of substitution, displacement, deferral, and

---

18. Mark Taylor, *Tears* (Albany: State University of New York Press, 1990), p. 203. Hereafter cited in the text as TR with appropriate page numbers.

difference. The disappearance of the self or the obscurity of the being of the self marks an epistemological undecidability in all of our thinking.

The deconstructive move that Taylor accepts is a move from principles to anarchy [Schurmann]. "Instead of an absolute origin (*arche*), the *an-arche*, which is *toujours-déjà*, renders impossible every origin and all originality" (TR, p. 44). This is a disaster and it is the recognition of this disaster that accounts for the affinity between Taylor's a/theological writing and Blanchot's *The Writing of the Disaster.* "The disaster 'reveals' nothing" (TC, p. 67). This is the nothing that philosophy and theology have left unthought. We crisscross this nothing between being and nonbeing in a/theological thinking. This nothing is marked in the interstices of a/theological writing. Resolution is refigured as dissolution. The task that Taylor has defined is to think and live the disaster of nothing.

In a *certain way* Taylor has inscribed silence on the body of theological thinking. It is a *way* of indirection, an erring. "[H]e writes a text of circuitous communiques in the language of the other" (EW, p. 130). He increasingly writes about postmodern visual arts, architecture, and literature as a way of writing a/theologically. That is, he entertains a fissured literature and a fissured practice to magnify the fissured textuality of a/theological thinking. He has understood Jabès: "Mark the first page of the book with a red marker. For, in the beginning, the wound is invisible."[19]

Does this mean that we have to mark the second page, the third page, and all of the rest of the pages with a red marker? Deconstructive a/theology has made the wound visible. This achievement is cathartic. What, however, follows the catharsis of radical criticism? There is certainly no prescriptive strategy that can be grounded in *an arche.* A deconstructive philosophical or theological agenda cannot be fixed. Deconstructive drift ceases to be itself if it is canalized. The most we can do is to analyze [loosen throughout] some of the ele-

19. Edmond Jabès, *The Book of Questions,* translated by Rosmarie Waldrop (Middletown: Wesleyan University Press, 1976), p. 13.

ments of a driftwork and see that these can be markings on a post-modern theological agenda. The first question that we might want to ask after reviewing Taylor's work is whether a/theology is theology. This is a variation on the earlier claim of a co-implication between theology and a postmodern sensibility. When we first glance at Taylor's a/theology, it appears to be fully theological because it lives parasitically on a theological host. Taylor repeats the Western theological tradition even if his intention is to make it tremble. This, however, is not a strong enough answer. The question is not whether a good thinker can do a deconstructive reading of theological literature. The question is whether theology has a deconstructive agenda and deconstruction has a theological agenda.

A clear, incisive, affirmative answer to this question is found in Scharlemann's essay, "The Being of God When God Is Not Being God." The coincidence between Taylor's a/theology and Scharlemann's theology is the valuation of alterity, a valuation of the "other" in the context of any discursive practice. As already noted, the thesis of this essay is that, "in the theological tradition, the otherness of God (the being of God when God is not being God, or the freedom of God both to be and not to be) has remained unthought and conceptually forgotten in exactly the same manner as has the question of the meaning of being" (DT, p. 88). The memory of this otherness in extreme theological formulations, such as Anselm's term for God in the ontological argument "that than which nothing greater can be conceived," instantiates within discourse an otherness that cannot be contained. "God means the negative that can be instantiated upon any object and any subject by the saying of the word. The word *instantiates* the negation—that is to say, it turns the subject by which it is spoken or the object to which it is applied into a sign of the subject's or object's own otherness" (DT, p. 88). Theology is a unique discourse when its basic terms are extreme formulations that naturally convolute the discourse. Theology and a/theology, when they are not forgetful of their own extreme formulations, are necessarily deconstructive.

The singularity of the deconstructive moment instantiating a radical negativity is not the whole of theological thinking. As Taylor noted, writing is a dissemination of meaning. In theological writing these figurations of extremity will dominate a discourse by pressuring the differential play of textual and intertextual referencing. Their assimilation into a discursive practice alters the already existing economy of the discourse. The traces of the other in the formulation of dominant theological concepts will manifest themselves in fissures, gaps, paradoxes, and incongruities throughout the discourse. These markings index the incompleteness of the movement toward totalization and, in this sense, violate or transgress any law of discursive closure.

Theology belongs to the population of all discursive practices. It remains text production. There is no special privilege to its discursive formations that comes from outside of the text production. The theological exigencies inscribed within its texts are effects of the metonymical placing of extreme formulations throughout the texts. The efficacy of these formulations is in their pressure upon ordinary usage and reference. The pressure of figurations of ultimacy on the pragmatics of discourse is a transvaluation of the ordinary. Formulations and figurations of ultimacy, when metonymically placed in a textual practice, can magnify the already existing fissures of received texts. The differential play of reference extends the witness to that which is other than the text through the incompleteness that is the result of the placement of these formulations. Theological texts explicitly express their internal undecidability. In this sense, theological texts introduce an incommensurability into discursive practices that is an internal trace of the other.

The very existence of theological thinking and writing implicates culture in a deconstructive practice. A/theology underlines the excesses of undecidability in theological thinking, but those excesses can seep into the larger population of discursive practices even when they are not explicitly recognized. The possibility for figurations of alterity is a point of resistance to any totalization of thought. The importance of theology and a/theology is that they are specific discursive practices that mark an exigency of mind, thus implicating all discursive practices in the other of language manifest in language. Taylor and Scharlemann explicitly mark this exigency of mind in their thinking. They are both concerned with the context that is other than the text even as they acknowledge that thinking is a discursive practice. There is an understanding that the context precedes and exceeds the text but is always thought textually. The context is always textualized while at the same time the text is always contextualized. We err in context but follow a text. This is an important difference, felt in tonality, between Taylor and Scharlemann. Following may be erring, but it is a special erring that involves a textual internalization of the other—the coincidence of what is exterior with what is most interior. Following is a textual exfoliation of the singularity of the call to follow. It is not a movement within the text, but it is a textual movement within the context. In Scharlemann's theology, it is a movement that can best be described as a dwelling that presupposes a context of peace. This presupposition is itself a text. It is an ontological presupposition that takes precedence over epistemology.

Taylor does not have confidence in the power of a "new being" or a new text to resolve an epistemological *aporia*. I think that this is why Taylor says that "[a]ltarity can be rendered—if at all—only in a text that is rent."[20] We can know the other only as an effect within a text. The other is not a text to be read. The context can fault the text; it can be textualized; but, it is not a text. Furthermore, the text can be faulted by intersecting an exteriority that resists textualization, interiorization, and subjective assimilation. We err in context in response to these intersections or singularities. Singularities are contingencies and not textual strategies. Even the call to follow, although textual, is a contingency within the discourse it intersects.

Erring and following are responses to the other of discourse as that other pressures the discourse in its incompleteness and often

20. Mark Taylor, *Disfiguring: Art, Architecture, Religion*, (Chicago: University of Chicago Press, 1992), p. 318. Hereafter cited in text as DAAR with appropriate page numbers.

along fissures or fault lines. Erring and following are, more important, moves in life and not just moves in discourse, although both of them may involve textual exfoliation in their actualization. The textual strategies work within textuality and textuality works within a context. Textual strategies such as disfiguring, deformation, defamiliarization, transcendental interrogation, and speculative augmentation keep texts from coming to closure. The rent text is permeable to its context. The work against completeness is always an experiment with the text. It does not determine the context. The work against completeness, a disfiguring, "enacts denegation in the realm of figure, image, form and representation" (DAAR, p. 7). The text is never a totality. The self as subjectivity is always unfinished.

Nine

Theology as a Minor Literature

> [A strategy] postulates a place that can be delimited as its own and serve as the base from which relations with an exteriority composed of targets or threats can be managed.
>
> By contrast with a strategy, a tactic is a calculated action determined by the absence of a proper locus. . . . The space of a tactic is the space of the other.
>
> Michel de Certeau, *The Practice of Everyday Life*

We have discussed multiple and diverse strategies for theological text production. One of our major concerns has been the strategic deracination of ordinariness. Can we have access to spheres of meaning and discourse that give importance to life? Can we liberate zones of intensity from common repression and experience new visibilities that give significance to meaning? These are very practical questions that we have been exploring primarily within a theoretical matrix. The discussion has assumed the proper place of a strategy in order to be developed.

When, however, we turn to the pragmatics of theological discursive practices we quickly discover that in a secular culture theology cannot easily delimit a *place* of its *own*. There is no sanctuary for theological reflection. The locus of a theology is the space of the other. This means that theology must be tactical as well as strategic. It must work within, through, and against the strategies of dominant discursive practices. It can be pragmatically characterized as a minor literature within a dominant discourse and vehicular language.[1] Strategic theological planning must be correlated with tactical implementation

---

1. See Gilles Deleuze and Felix Guattari, *Kafka: Towards a Minor Literature,* translated by Dana Polan (Minneapolis: University of Minnesota Press, 1986), for the development and characteristics of a minor literature in their analysis of Kafka's use of German against German. Hereafter cited in the text as KL with appropriate page numbers.

if we are pragmatically and existentially concerned with the strategic goals and also recognize that theology does not have a proper place of its own. Certain recognitions are required for theology to function with both strategic and tactical efficacy. First, theology cannot posture as the "queen" of the sciences. It has a marginal status in contemporary discourse and it needs to recognize that its strategic formulations are worked out in the margins and interstices of the dominant culture. Movements into the mainstream of the culture are tactical implementations and experimentations. Second, within theological thinking at the close of the twentieth century there are competing hypotheses but there are no dominant paradigms to internally define theology as a science. Even definitions of religion and theology are in dispute. There are certainly no agreed-upon first principles for theological thinking. There are, instead, assemblages of ideas, epochal arrangements, and conflicting interpretations. Epistemic undecidability has unmoored the philosophical, linguistic, and social scientific foundations of theology, thus setting it adrift. Third, the dominant discourse of exchange is materialistic. That is, the economy is the dominant sector of society and shapes its primary values. What is meaningful is generally understood within a dominant discourse of the commodification of values. This dominant discourse is vehicular, the vehicle for the exchange and establishment of power. Fourth, a text, even the text of a dominant discourse, is never a totality. There are spaces, even when there are not proper places, for thinking, speaking, and writing other than in the style of the dominant discourse. These spaces are the possibility for developing a minor literature within a major or dominant discourse.

The need for a minor literature is to resist the repressive totalizing tendencies of the dominant discourse that seeks to stabilize itself in the midst of its incompleteness. We need a discourse that seeks no advantage by eliding destabilizing singularities of experience from its own register if we are to experience the intensity of singular experiences and the exfoliation of meaning that flows from them. In particular, conceiving of theology as a minor literature is a tactical implementation of the multiple strategies of acoluthetic reason, erring, deconstructive and hermeneutical tropologies, bricolage, radical criticism, parabolic and paradoxical narratives in the context of a dominant discourse of commodification. A minor literature is made of texts that are unsafe and are a contagion that makes all texts unsafe. Minor literatures teach us to stammer in our own language.[2] The strategies articulated here fall generally into two categories. There are topological strategies and tropological strategies. The topological strategies prepare surfaces for the recording or marking of theological texts. The tropological strategies are strategies of experimentation, intervention, transgression, convolution, and fissuring. These, however, are not exclusive categories. Topological and tropological strategies often overlap, sometimes coincide, and always contribute to each other.

Topological strategies are directed toward the construction of surfaces of inscription that are complex and highly variegated when theology seeks to attend to the diverse heterogeneities of experience. Can theology construct and frame a surface so that a singularity can be thought in the frame of its occurrence? Are the theological surfaces complex enough so that singularities can be indexed as surface effects? Topological strategies are investments in the possibility for thinking the given intensities, fluxes, flows, pulsions, and empiricities of context. Surfaces can be cultivated by rhetorical interrogations, metaphorical elaborations, and metonymical assemblages. Topological strategies are employed to make material space for the marking and remarking of singularities.

Topological strategies are often formed following the catharsis of radical criticism. Critical thinking notes the inadequacies of a frame and constrictions of the recording surface that elide singularities from further consideration. What is noted is the fleeting presence of an absence, a trace of the other. Something is lost. What is noted is that experience is diminished by simplifying recording surfaces and regularizing the frames of discourse. For examples, defining being as

---

2. Gilles Deleuze and Claire Parnet, *Dialogues,* translated by Hugh Tomlinson and Barbara Habberjam (New York: Columbia University Press, 1987), p. 4. Hereafter cited in the text as DP with appropriate page numbers.

presence or the self as subjectivity are too conceptually simplistic for framing and indexing the heterogeneities of experience. In contrast, the critical displacement of the subject is not a loss of the subject but a complexification of the subject that extends the recording surface of experience.

Extending the recording surface of experience is not just a commitment to brute fact. In the intersection of multiple discourses, it is also a commitment to being marked by the excluded voices of discourses that are other than itself. Topographical strategies are strategies for the liberation of excluded voices. They are strategies for contact and exchange, revision and emergence, as well as for marking nondiscursive singularities.

As noted, theological text production is also tropological. As a secondary process of thinking, theology is able to intervene in its own production, fissure its recording surface, and witness to what is other than its representations by elaborating its own incompleteness. This is not the same as being marked by a singularity. The singularity is received into the enigma of representational processes. The discourse is marked from outside of its ordered structure. The singularity disrupts the containment of any particular discursive practice. Thus, an enigma is noted. Tropological strategies seek to articulate the enigma by disrupting discourse from within its practice. The enigma is presupposed or inferred from the breakdown of ordinary discursive practices.

What Derrida calls *différance* is one name for the enigma of representational processes. Coming to representation is a work of substitution of an image/sign for the nondiscursive reality that has come to representation. It is a process of differing that is always also a deferral of presence. Derrida in continuity with Heidegger recognizes that in the representational economy of secondary process thinking, identity is difference. Representations can never be anything other than simulacra. The "other" of discourse ceases to be itself when it is in discourse. The "other" in discourse is a disturbance, crack, fissure, or gap in the representational economy. The "other" in discourse is discourse in ecstasy. Discourse is inhabited by a nonidentity, a moment of deterritorialization, an internal silence.

Tropological strategies suggest intentional moves within secondary process thinking. These are moves within a representational economy. These are moves that place images, words, and phrases in contestation. These moves fault the text. They make the text unsafe from inside of its differential play. As was discussed in chapter 7, tropological strategies are diverse and multiple. There is no one set of such strategies.

There can be critical interventions in existing textual practices attending to traces of alterity within texts. Texts are fissured by their moments of exclusion made visible by criticism. These critical interventions are common practices of deconstructive theologies, feminist theologies, and liberation theologies. There can also be the experimental generation of fissured texts as we see in the more playful writings of Derrida or Deleuze and Guattari.[3] These texts pressure the meaning of text and textuality. There can also be a reversal of narrative in parable. Text production is then paradoxical. All of these moves intentionally problematize the relationship between text and context.

No texts are isolated, self-sufficient, or self-authorized. No text can be self-enclosed. Texts are always an unfinished business. Even a dominant discourse can never fully secure its boundaries or completely repress its genealogy. It is this permeability to context that is the possibility for the development of minor literatures.

Textuality and intertextuality are differential plays of signification. The determinant meaning of any signifier is its relationship to other signifiers. The signified is itself a signifier. Iterability and reiterability mean that all collective assemblages of enunciation are always vulnerable to new processes of signification. Texts have a dialectical vulnerability when they intersect each other. There is an ongoing emergent textuality that can be either evolutionary or revolutionary. Textual isolation and repression of other textual practices are strategies that attempt to deny the possibilities for emergent tex-

---

3. For example, see Jacques Derrida, *Glas,* translated by John P. Leavey, Jr., and Richard Rand (Lincoln: University of Nebraska Press, 1986); or Gilles Deleuze and Felix Guattari, *A Thousand Plateaus: Capitalism and Schizophrenia,* translated by Brian Massumi (Minneapolis: University of Minnesota Press, 1987).

tuality but they can never be completely successful because, for texts to be what they are, they are already weighted with a complex association of meanings. They are in language and there are no private languages. Making sense is referentially and intertextually overdetermined by the ongoing play of signifiers. This is what is meant by sense in the secondary process thinking of conscious deliberation.

A discourse can be dominant but never final. There is no final sense. No particular discourse can control its own use in another discursive practice. It is not simply that there are conflicts of interpretation. The rules for the formation of a discursive practice, frames and recording surfaces, can be altered so that when the discourse is reinscribed it is a different discourse with new contours and in a new differential context. Its meaning is insecure. That is, secondary process thinking is insecure on the register of secondary process thinking. Necessary and constant deferral means that nothing is ever settled.

Of course, the contexts of a text are not just simply texts. All texts are always already a part of existing discursive contexts, but there are also nondiscursive contexts for all discourses. This distinction correlates with the distinction that we have been using between secondary and primary process thinking and further complicates the relationship between text and context. Consciousness is not nothing and it is not everything. Derrida's nonconcept *différance,* Kristeva's *transversal negativity,* and Freud's *primal repression* are negative notations or traces of a primary process thinking that is nondiscursive.

There are also secondary elaborations within discourse that seek to simulate what is other than discourse. These simulacra cathect the primary process but are never identical with it. Force, power, the unconscious, the semiotic chora, assemblages of desire, pulsions, fluxes are valuations more than descriptions of a context that is other than discourse. This context is a matrix for the production of identity. It is a matrix of objective appearance that is not in-itself thought in objective appearances. We are talking about a schema of productivity and not the production. The simulacra of force index markings of the effects of force on the surface of secondary process thinking rather than know the primary matrix. Descriptions and elaborations of primary process thinking are simply moves to implicate the whole of discursive practices in their nondiscursive context. In a different idiom and with a different ambience, we are remarking Jean-Paul Sartre's claim that "in the face of the dazzling night of Being, consciousness, which is comedy, which is fake, which is makeshift, a coming to terms with self because it has to make itself be what it is, discovers a type of pitiless being without compromises or accommodations, the absolute and irremediable necessity of being what we are—forever and beyond all changes."[4] Freedom and consciousness, discursive manifestations of secondary process thinking, are situated in the context of the incorrigibility of the body and all of its material filiations.

Discursive and nondiscursive multiplicities prevent the successful idealization and isolation of the text. Force and meaning intersect in the representational process and meaning is secondary. Thinking, speaking, and writing are embedded and implicated in a material nexus of forces that are quasi-transcendental conditions for discourse. This context is not a content. It is not a text. Nothing is ever settled.

It is the ever unsettled reality of text production that allows us to rethink strategic planning tactically. There are always spaces, discursive and nondiscursive spaces, that, although they are not sanctioned or proper to a dominant discourse, can be inhabited by theological interrogations. I am suggesting that theology can insinuate itself into the dominant culture.

This is what I mean by the tactical use of theological strategies. These tactics are not new strategies. Tactics are the use value of strategies of resistance in a dominant secular culture. It is because theology does not have a proper place of its own in the dominant secular culture that it must value and affirm its identity as a marginal and intersticial reality. That is, theology inhabits the edges and cracks of the dominant culture. It is a nomad discipline wandering, wondering, and erring.

4. Jean-Paul Sartre, *Truth and Existence,* translated by Adrian van den Hoven (Chicago: University of Chicago Press, 1992), pp. 45–46.

The tactical use of theological strategies is not unlike what Michel de Certeau calls the tactics of consumption in the practice of everyday life.[5] He recognizes that marginality is becoming a universal phenomenon among the consumers and nonproducers of the dominant culture (PEL, p. xvii). Consumers make use of what they are given in ways that serve their own ends. Tactics insinuate uses in the space of the other. Ends are turned by new uses. The text of the dominant culture is troped so that it is usable in a style other than it has intended itself. De Certeau describes this process as a political act in which the "weak" make use of the "strong" and subvert the dominant culture without ever overcoming it. They make a space for themselves within the constraints imposed on them. Their "making do" is an undoing of totalizing claims and moves toward closure in the dominant culture. The dominant text is thereby mutated. "This mutation makes the text habitable, like a rented apartment. It transforms another person's property into a space borrowed for a moment by a transient. . . . [T]he procedures of contemporary consumption appear to constitute a subtle art of 'renters' who know how to insinuate their countless differences into the dominant text" (PEL, pp. xxi–xxii).

Since theologians do not have a proper place in the dominant culture they, like other marginalized consumers, must rent their space. They must insinuate their differences into the dominant text. Theological strategies are efficacious to the extent that they can be tactically insinuated into existing textual practices. Tactics exploit the discursive and nondiscursive spacing in the dominant discourse. A minor literature is generated inside and alongside of the dominant discourse, metonymically pressuring its continual formation. New lines and surfaces complicate the dominant discourse. The dominant discourse goes outside of itself inside of itself.

Theology claims a relevance when it is a minor intensive use of a major language. It is not a segregated literature of an isolated com-

5. See Michel de Certeau, *The Practice of Everyday Life*, translated by Steven Rendall (Berkeley: University of California Press, 1984), General Introduction and Part I. Hereafter cited in the text as PEL with appropriate page numbers.

munity that privileges itself as culturally separate and, often, ironically irrelevant to how people experience their lives as real and important. A minor intensive theological literature is not a "Sunday-school" theology. It inhabits spaces in the weave of everyday discourses. It insinuates formulations of extremity into the fissures of ordinary discourse, thereby generating an extraordinary discourse. What emerges is something akin to what Huston Smith calls divine ordinariness in his understanding of Zen Buddhism.[6] Theology acts on the ordinariness of a dominant discourse and transforms its experiential meaning.

In generally characterizing minor literatures, Deleuze and Guattari note that they affect the dominant discourse with a high coefficient of deterritorialization (KL, p. 16). The settled order is unsettled. Use functions are redirected. There are new trajectories, new lines of filiation in the signifying play of discourse. This means that there are new fault lines, new openings or spaces within the discourse. The discourse is rendered increasingly permeable to the flux of the "real." "Writing always combines with something else, which is its own becoming. There is no assemblage which functions on a single flux" (DP, p. 44). Becomings are affairs of primary and secondary process thinking. Developing a minor intensive literature is an investment in this complexity. It is a recognition and investment in the incorrigibilities of both the mind and the body. Thinking exceeds its representational economy. Becomings are formations of power as well as representational assemblages of meaning.

Minor literatures are political (KL, pp. 17–18). They are pragmatically bound to acts of deterritorialization and reterritorialization. They are pragmatically bound to new becomings that are also configurations of power and language in the complex relationship of primary and secondary process thinking. They mark zones of intensity that risk the established order. They open spaces for forces to pressure the articulation of order in any representational economy.

These are all pragmatic considerations within the politics of lan-

---

6. See Huston Smith, *The World's Religions* (San Francisco: Harper and Row, 1991), p. 137.

guage. We are asking how a minor literature functions in relationship to a dominant discourse. Strategies may be concerned with content, but tactics are concerned with applications. Strategies are concerned with marking and opening discourse to the "other" of discourse. Tactics are concerned with marking and opening a literary space for theological thinking when it has no proper place in the dominant culture. Sometimes strategic and tactical planning and their resultant moves are not discernably different. What is required of tactical thinking is an evaluation of the status and function of theological thinking. For example, understanding theology as a minor literature is a tactical valuation of theological strategies. An element of the "subtle renter's art" is the recognition that you are a renter.

Tactics are concerned with specific locations and regional assemblages of power. Tactics without strategies for theological text production would be meaningless, and strategies without tactics for theological text placement would be irrelevant. Something must be said [written] and something must be heard [read].

Theological tactical thinking exploits the strategic deracination of ordinariness. Tactics seek to make large natural fissures in discourse and amplify voices of the "other" of the dominant discourse. Tactical thinking is necessarily allied with the critique of culture and is often located in the metonymical "and" of religion and culture, religion and psychology, religion and society, religion and ethics, religion and politics. It is an extended implementation of the making "unsafe" of the cultural texts that order our thinking.

It is not as if there ever were safe texts and secure communities that can be threatened by the development of minor literatures. The possible existence of minor literatures in general and the extreme formulations of theology in particular are a recognition that texts are never safe and that self, community, and society are always at risk. They are always unfinished. They are always in the making.

Theology as a minor literature is a liberating social text. Marking the "other" of discourse disenfranchises language's oppressive qualities. The dominant discourse cannot make itself safe. There is little advantage to eliding singularities or defining zones of intensity as zones of abjection to secure a text that is already unsafe.

The pragmatics of theological discourse is an applied recognition of the epistemic undecidability underlying all discourse. This epistemic undecidability was theologically instantiated in singular experiences of speaking the "name of God," proclaiming the "death of God," or articulating other formulations of "that than which nothing greater can be conceived." Theology can be a constant undoing of the totalization of any particular discourses, even theological discourses, when it understands itself as a minor literature. The minor intensive use of language opposes the "oppressed quality" of language to its "oppressive quality" (KL, p. 27).

Theological thinking makes openings for rethinking self, community, and society. Ordinariness too often has been a compromise with the claims of unfounded totalized texts that exclude the "other" of and in discourse. Ordinariness too often has been the satisfaction of feeling familiar with a world that is constricted by the oppressive quality of language. These feelings are too easy and too empty. They lack intensity and importance.

We began our inquiry with the felt loss of intensity and importance. Can this loss be confronted by theology? The answer has been "yes," when theology is willing to adopt deracinating strategies and tactically employ itself as a minor literature. What is the importance of this "yes?" How does the "yes" to theology and the "yes" of theology implicate us in a newly articulated community?

Ten

Desiring Community

*Oh, those Greeks! They knew how to live. What is required for that is
to stop courageously at the surface, the fold, the skin, to adore appearance, to believe in forms, tones, words . . . Those Greeks were superficial
out of profundity.*

Friedrich Nietzsche, *The Gay Science*

*O the generations of men the dying generations—adding the total of all
your lives I find they come to nothing.*

Sophocles, *Oedipus the King*

*Stop, my children, weep no more. Here where the dark forces store up
kindness both for the living and the dead, there is no room for grieving
here—*

Sophocles, *Oedipus at Colonus*

At the beginning of this inquiry, the question was posed whether
the surfaces of experience can give way to the depths. That
question must now be reconfigured in response to the theoretical
considerations of epistemic undecidability that have dominated our
discussion. Why does Nietzsche say the Greeks were superficial out
of their profundity and how can Sophocles say weep no more after
saying that life means nothing? These questions press upon a secular culture out of an insistent sense of finitude that is the only credible sense of reality after serious reflection on the experience of what
it means to be human. The experience of originality without origins
and serious thinking without foundations keeps us bound to surfaces that are the space and theater of meaning. The metaphor of
depth continues to have meaning but it is now measured in a language of surface complexity. Depth is a complex inscription on the
recording surface of experience. It can also be a valuation of the
complexity of the recording surface itself.

Depth is achieved topologically and tropologically. There is a certain adequation between becoming deep and becoming complex. Thinking is a dissemination of meaning across surfaces. It is a work of becoming that can know joy in the aesthetic satisfaction of increasingly complex differential arrangements. This is a constitutive complexity in which, as Whitehead suggested, "[t]he many become one and are increased by one."[1] Creativity, the making and dissemination of meaning, is a work within the disjunctive diversity and heterogeneity of events and forces that are the material context of experience. Creativity is itself an event of epochal arrangement.

The strategies and tactics of a secular postmodern theology are a continuing experiment in epochal arrangement that has no privileged access to first principles or origins that are outside of its own making. Theology remains text production and in this sense it is not archeology. It can only authenticate itself within its own making. That theology, or any other thinking, can only simulate first principles need not be a cause of despair.

I began this chapter with quotations expressing the dark vision of Greek tragedy because they are exemplary of a vision of finitude that goes beyond despair. Even if our lives come to nothing, there is a transformation in the Sophoclean vision of the dark forces so that they store up kindness. There is in this vision a meaning to surfaces that Nietzsche also comes to celebrate. Pierre Vidal-Naquet remarks that "*Oedipus at Colonus* is a tragedy about passages from one point to another. . . . this is a tragedy about frontiers, frontiers that separate people but also frontiers that enable them to come together."[2] What is the space of a frontier that enables people to come together? What is the power and gift of Oedipus?

As witnessed by the Chorus in *Oedipus at Colonus*, "but now one's come, the rumors say who fears the Furies not at all—"[3] Oedi-

---

1. Alfred North Whitehead, *Process and Reality: Corrected Edition,* edited by David Ray Griffin and Donald W. Sherburne (New York: The Free Press, 1978), p. 21.
2. Jean-Pierre Vernant and Pierre Vidal-Naquet, *Myth and Tragedy in Ancient Greece,* translated by Janet Lloyd (New York: Zone Books, 1988), p. 359.
3. Sophocles, *The Three Theban Plays,* translated by Robert Fagles (New York: Penguin Books, 1984), p. 291. Hereafter cited in the text as TT with appropriate page numbers.

pus is able to walk and talk on forbidden ground and the Chorus asks him to "move off forbidden ground, come down where the law permits us all to speak" (TT, p. 292). The Furies are our finitude and Oedipus is not afraid to recognize and speak of that finitude. Through his suffering he has an understanding that he can give as a gift to Theseus. He is able to speak and listen with "no more fighting with necessity" (TT, p. 294). He is able to reveal to Theseus "the power that age cannot destroy, the heritage stored for you [Theseus] and Athens" (TT, p. 375). Theseus can say of Oedipus at his death, "he was content that all was done, and of all he wanted, nothing more was needed, nothing left to do" (TT, p. 379).

That our lives come to nothing is transvalued when nothing more is needed, nothing left to do. The *nothing* is transvalued. The *something* of life can be valued because *nothing* more is needed. There is here an affirmation of necessity that Nietzsche will later call *amor fati*. "I want to learn more and more to see as beautiful what is necessary in things; then, I shall be one of those who makes things beautiful."[4]

What appears in the history of philosophy as strange and exaggerated metaphysical formulations, Nietzsche's own doctrine of eternal recurrence, Leibniz's "best of all possible worlds," and Whitehead's ontological principle, are all an insistence on finitude and function ethically in the valuation of necessity, *amor fati*. Much philosophy and theology as I am conceiving of it will function ethically in experimental constructions and differential arrangements that enable us to speak even on the ground of the Furies. Not only do we want to be able to speak on these grounds, but we also need to consent to the reality that it is on these grounds that we must make community, culture, and civilization. We cannot wish away the necessity of our finitude and inevitability of our death. Since finite life is what we experience, in an ironic turn it must be valued and cared for as finite. To not be able to will the eternal recurrence of the same is a

---

4. Friedrich Nietzsche, *The Gay Science,* translated by Walter Kaufmann (New York: Vintage Books, 1974), p. 223. Hereafter cited in the text as GS with appropriate page numbers.

devaluation and a repression of life. Nietzsche regarded the notion of eternal recurrence as the greatest weight that can either crush us or confirm us in our existence (GS, pp. 273–74).

There is always a danger that we will choose to negate life with the false consciousness that a negation of the negativity in finitude will be an affirmation. There are strategies in thinking of totalization that seek to mask or deny the transitoriness, contingency, and relativity that characterize the experience of finitude. It is this tendency toward repressive totalization that is resisted by the strategies and tactics of theological thinking as I have conceived of them. This means that self and community will have to be thought in other than a deontological or ontotheological frame. There is no settled reality, first principles, or safe texts that can guarantee the security or quality of life together or the meaningfulness of the self's becoming.

This does not mean that we cannot form communities, choose principles, and write and value texts. Epistemic undecidability does not prevent or even inhibit ethical decidability. It simply shifts the responsibility for ethical and political decision making into an experimental and pragmatic frame of conscious freedom. It is a work of becoming, becoming self and becoming community. These becomings are always at risk and sometimes fragile. They are subject to diverse singularities that intersect their projects and multiple forces that are their context. The becomings of community are vulnerable to the freedom and valuations of those that are other than the community. Communities can become inoperative in a conflict of interpretation or valuation. They can break down even over misunderstood words. What is at stake is that self becoming is always relational (communal), always contingent, and always unfinished. Both the self and the community are works against completeness. There are no borders that are ever finalized. As becoming, being and thinking are always heuristic. We are here in agreement with Sartre that "obviously we have to be our own hypothesis."[5]

---

5. Jean-Paul Sartre, *Truth and Existence*, translated by Adrian van den Hoven (Chicago: University of Chicago Press, 1992), p. 15. Hereafter cited in the text as TE with appropriate page numbers.

This is, of course, not always easy. We are a hypothesis in context. In the context of finitude, "[t]o want the truth is to prefer Being to anything else, even in a catastrophic form, simply because it *is*" (TE, p. 30). This is a movement against Descartes's hypothesis of the self as subjectivity and Hegel's totalization of this hypothesis in the notion of absolute subjectivity. The absolute is relativized as a construct in the process of becoming. In processes of becoming absolute, formulations can only function metaphorically or metonymically as elements within the process. There is not a truth to be found but a truth to be made in the process. We can note an affinity between Sartre's making things true and Nietzsche's making things beautiful that bears upon the possibility for meaningful community.

They are both talking about valuing life in its finite presentation. The metaphysical question, "Why is there something rather than nothing?" is transformed into an ethical affirmation or valuation that there is something. Neither of them were seeking the ignorance that is an escape from reality but that also often will masquerade as a deeper reality. The risk that the hypotheses of self and community will unravel in their becomings does not justify a false consciousness of totalized formulations. The construction and choice of an illusion is a work against life and a devaluation of necessity.

Of course, no one would choose to order life by an illusion knowing that it is an illusion. It is not that we simply choose an illusion. We instead can choose a critical silence that lets constructions within the differential play of conscious thinking hide or repress the various intensities, empiricities, singularities, and forces that press on us. The Chorus in *Oedipus at Colonus*, when referring to the grove of the Furies, says, "Oh we tremble to say their names, filing by, not a look, not a sound, not a word moving our lips in silence" (TT, p. 291). In contrast, Oedipus could walk and talk in the grove of the Furies. His gift was a blessing for Athenian civilization. It would appear that the meaning of the hermeneutics of suspicion is a similar blessing.

It is precisely to be able to overcome a silence about life and its finite entailments that I have sought to develop a secular mandate for theology. We want to be able to talk about life in the critical wake of the hermeneutics of suspicion. We want to be able to speak of life without denying or repressing the great forces *Eros, Thanatos,* and *Ananke* as well as attend to the many particularities that constitute the context of our becoming. This speaking requires ongoing radical criticism and interrogation of all conceptual formulations. Radical criticism is, in this perspective, an ethical formulation and a possibility for meaningful community.

It is a radical critique that reveals to us how precarious are the becomings of self and community. It is a radical critique that reveals how much we must care for the other in and of language as primary elements in our own becoming. And, it is a radical critique that opens thinking to the singularities of experience that can fill and delight us.

The ethical thinking that I am here formulating might best be thought of as a paraethics or parapolitics, an ethics beside itself and a politics beside itself.[6] Paraethics is an ethics of indirection. It would be contrasted with an ethics that understands itself as based on first principles. Epistemic undecidability in our discursive practices works against the credibility of traditional ethical thinking. We can no longer develop an ethic in itself and that is why I am proposing an ethic beside itself. Paraethics is an implementation of the strategies and tactics of theological thinking. We can even say that it is an implication of those strategies and tactics.

The deconstructive force of theological thinking is a continuous pressure against the totalization and closure of a dominant discourse. That is, it works against any valuation of an ideology that is a devaluation of the complex heterological infrastructure of the dynamics of becoming. Without explicitly identifying itself as an ethic, it has ethical implications. Theology opens spaces for an otherness in discourse and for an otherness of discourse simply by the inscription of the name of God, other formulations of extremity, or even naming the death of God. The voice of the other and experience of otherness cannot be excluded when any and every particular discourse is denied

---

6. I first encountered the notion of paraethics in a seminar paper by Victor Taylor of the Humanities Doctoral Program of Syracuse University.

closure. The other of discourse is neither necessarily good nor benign. But, it is in the context of becoming. It has the necessity of being reality. If we try to formally exclude the otherness of reality from the becomings of self and community, both are diminished in the intensity of their satisfaction and both are precariously subject to a return of the repressed.

There is a tension in these insights that resonates with a tension in the later works of Sigmund Freud, especially *The Future of an Illusion* and *Civilization and Its Discontents.*[7] "We are threatened with suffering from three directions: from our own body, which is doomed to decay and dissolution and which cannot even do without pain and anxiety as warning signals; from the external world, which may rage against us with overwhelming and merciless forces of destruction; and finally from our relations to other men [*sic*]" (PWSF, p. 77). It is even possible that "[l]ife, as we find it, is too hard for us; it brings us too many pains, disappointments and impossible tasks" (PWSF, p. 75). Does the incorrigibility of mind, an excess of subjectivity in a finite context, always mean a fleeting loss of intensity and satisfaction? What must we give up to survive? Is it possible to mate intensity with survival? Whitehead articulates this as "the problem for Nature."[8] The becomings of self and community are situated in civilization with its discontents.

Freud suggests that in order to bear life we need palliative measures or auxiliary constructions. He mentions three such measures: "powerful deflections, which cause us to make light of our misery; substitutive satisfactions, which diminish it; and intoxicating substances, which make us insensitive to it" (PWSF, p. 75). These are all measures that seek to influence our own organism and particularly the experience of our subjectivity. They all fail to address the incorrigibility and constitutive complexity of the becoming of the body. In

---

7. Sigmund Freud, *The Standard Edition of the Complete Psychological Works of Sigmund Freud,* 24 vols. translated by James Strachey (London: The Hogarth Press, 1961), vol. XXI. Hereafter cited in the text as PWSF with appropriate page numbers.

8. "Thus the problem for Nature is the production of societies which are 'structured' with a high 'complexity,' and which are at the same time 'unspecialized.' In this way, intensity is mated with survival." (Whitehead, *Process and Reality,* p. 101.)

particular, deflection and substitution tend toward totalization to secure their credibility as sources of satisfaction. A move toward a totalizing intoxication would be a move toward death. Ironically, intoxication privileges the body while destroying it. Deflection and substitution privilege the experience of mind while closing it. Deflection and substitution are actions of a secondary process thinking that depend on a primal repression and substitution they cannot control. The palliatives of deflection and substitution are in discourse. They are discursive practices. They are ways of writing the identity of the self and ways of writing the text of the world. They are always simulations. As a defense against suffering their purpose is a forgetfulness of the pain of finitude. Their satisfactions may be transitionally psychologically effective, but the pain that they hide comes back.

The simulacra and apparatus of psychological defense is haunted by Sophocles' Chorus. "Not to be born is best when all is reckoned in, but once a man has seen the light the next best thing by far, is to go back where he came from, quickly as he can. For once his youth slips by . . . what mortal blows can he escape—what griefs won't stalk his days" (TT, p. 358). The passage into disease and old age and the inexorable reality of death undo the efficacy of provisional psychological solutions. A safe text of life without risk and without being subject to diverse finite forces is an illusion.

We return to the question as to whether other arrangements for living are possible. How might they look? This is a societal as well as an individual or psychological question. The auxiliary constructions that Freud understands psychologically can and are also elaborated societally and politically. Individual illusion is elaborated as mass delusion. Strategies that construct the self through a repression of otherness often become societally elaborated as strategies for the oppression and disenfranchisement of others. Thinking can be a discursive practice that marks off territories that give no space to the other. Even more disturbing are the irredentist aspirations of a totalizing thought that are making claims to the space of the other. Ethnic cleansing, genocide, and deportation are just some of the macropolitical expressions of how totalizing discursive practices can and have been elaborated. Totalization depends on a claim of normativity, and it is precisely this claim that can be paraethically challenged.

Paraethics is, first of all, a radical critique that is practiced in the belief that life is less beautiful when people are oppressed and disenfranchised, when nature is exploited and despoiled, and when the diverse singularities of life are denied recognition and exfoliation. It is, second of all, a radical critique practiced in the belief that, most important, it is the securing of a totalizing thinking as a dominant discourse that is the mechanism for making life less beautiful.

In a late-capitalist society, this dominant discourse appears to be a materialist commodification of values with its ideology elaborated primarily and efficaciously through advertising. However, it could be a Marxist discourse, a Stalinist discourse, a Nazi discourse, or a fundamentalist discourse of religion that is challenged by paraethical thinking. What is *ethical* is certainly not always what is good or what is beautiful. A dominant discourse often practices in its normativity an ethics of exclusion to secure its privilege. As in all discursive practices, the texts of the dominant discourse are unsafe and it is this reality that the discourse seeks to deny.

Theology, as a minor literature, is a paraethics. It is a nomadic discipline wandering about the margins and through the interstices of the dominant discourse, making it consciously unsafe. Whatever are its formulations of "that than which nothing greater can be conceived," they will function as deconstructive levers in the dominant discourse as they continue to metonymically pressure the dominant discourse's continuing formulations. Paraethics is deconstructive as it works beside the normative ethics of the dominant discourse. It is making conceptual space for the other of experience and the experience of the other.

Paraethics is a permanent as well as a radical critique, a continual interrogation of the constructs of experience and their valuation. The extreme formulations of theological thinking can act as an ethical imperative in unsettling the stability of how things are. Nietzsche's question, lodged in the doctrine of eternal recurrence, "Do you desire this once more and enumerable times more?" pressures the valuation of any experience by extending it eternally (GS, p. 274). Tillich's question, lodged in the definition of faith as ultimate concern, "What do you take seriously without any reservation?" pressures the valuation of any experience by extending it into a context of ultimacy. The question is whether finite constructions can maintain their claim of a totalizing prerogative when they abut formulations of extremity. The force of theology as paraethics is the instantiation of a radical negativity that deconstructs totalizing discourses. We could say that in this first paraethical phase, theology is a deterritorializing textual violence. This is primarily the work of a hermeneutical tropology.

However, this is a meaningful work in the sphere of paraethics only because of the topological preparation of recording surfaces. Tropological disfiguration is an opening for the inscription of alterities on an elaborated text that is itself prepared to be open to the heterological infrastructure of becoming. Relativizing the dominant discourse lifts a veil of repression within the secondary constructs of thinking or, perhaps it is better to say, the discourse is loosened throughout. The effects of contextual forces can be marked within experience as can the multiple contingent singularities that intersect processes of becoming. Release and recognition characterize the second paraethical phase.

This phase has resonance both with Heidegger's understanding of the donative power of language, "to say" is "to show, to make appear, the lighting-concealing-releasing offer of the world," and with Nietzsche's injunction, "You shall become the person you are."[9] The deconstructive work against repression and totalization has opened spaces on the surface of inscription for marking and disclosure of what is already there. We can realize ourselves in the truth of own becomings. We can choose the satisfaction of the complexity of life.

Choosing is a third phase. Epistemic undecidability here gives way to ethical decidability. Ethical decidability is a valuation of peo-

---

9. Martin Heidegger, *On the Way Toward Language*, translated by Peter D. Hertz (New York: Harper & Row, 1971), p. 107; and Nietzsche, *Gay Science*, p. 219.

ple, things, events, and forces that come to appear within the discursive frames on the surface of consciousness. These discursive frames are perspectives that are never absolute. We are confronted with an ever-changing kaleidoscope of appearances. These are the intensities, empiricities, and singularities that we know as our world. We have accessed this world through a deconstructive topology and tropology. We are now and we are continually confronted with an ethical demand to value positively or negatively what has come to appear. In our own becoming we choose the meaning of importance. Importance is our responsibility.

The extreme formulation of a positive finite valuation is what we know as love. In *Civilization and Its Discontents*, Freud describes love as a technique in the art of living that "does not turn away from the external world; on the contrary, it clings to the objects belonging to that world and obtains happiness from an emotional relationship to them" (PWSF, pp. 81–82). It is not surprising that Freud understands sexual love as providing a pattern for the meaning of love in the search for happiness and intense satisfaction. It is on this path that we first encounter happiness. The question is why anyone would ever abandon this path or technique for living. Freud answers: "It is that we are never so defenceless against suffering as when we love, never so helplessly unhappy as when we have lost our loved object or its love" (PWSF, p. 82).

The intense valuation of the other in love "offers finitude in its truth."[10] We are totally vulnerable because love is radically contingent, subject to the will of the other, and subject to the will of the Furies. We *can* lose our loved object or its love. To be in love is to always be at risk. In love, the processes of becoming self and becoming community are intensely experienced as internally related. The controlled I think and I am of the *cogito* is ecstatically transcended by an I am I because I am loved and I love.

One of the problems with love is that we don't love in general

---

10. Cf. Jean-Luc Nancy, *The Inoperative Community*, translated by Peter Connor, Lisa Garbus, Michael Holland, and Simona Sawhney (Minneapolis: University of Minnesota Press, 1991), p. 99.

and cannot be safe in the totalizing claims of the generality of love. Love for humanity is an empty formulation. Love is particular and singular. There can be multiple singular experiences of love, but they are always specific and contingent on place and time. Love is an intense valuation of specificities in the finite display of experience. It is precisely because finite experience is highly variegated that the "yes" to the importance of any specific person or object is meaningful. In love, we are making life meaningful, but it is a meaning that can be neither contained nor controlled. Love makes life unsafe. This is its frightening and wonderful transformational power.

There are no texts that can protect love and no language of avowal that can guarantee its future. Discursive practices can enunciate love, exfoliate love, and disseminate love. There are also discursive practices that repress love. When a discourse denies the truth of finitude, it denies love. It denies the truth of love in the repression of difference. Identity in difference is a condition for love. It is a condition for all becoming that is consciously recognized in the valuation that is love. Lovers know that their identity as "loved" is constituted in a differential relationship with their lover. They will usually try to protect the specificity of this relationship and not squander its importance and meaning. The discourse of love has to work against discourses of repression to be itself.

The discourse of love has an important affinity with the deconstructive tropology of theology. The affinity is so important that it will help describe meaningful possibilities for a theologically informed community. Love can become a transformational contagion. It has to recognize the singularity of its origination to exfoliate itself in joy. Its discourse requires an openness to singularities and other intensities of experience. It is vulnerable not only to loss but is also open to gain in experience. The child that experiences love can risk an openness to the world. Romantic lovers often discover that their world has been transformed. The contingencies that are indexed on the trajectory of their love, a taverna where they first met, a shabby apartment, a city, are specifically valued with a different intensity. The world in its finite display is given importance in the lovers' discourse.

The affinity between the lovers' discourse and theological thinking is the joy in the becoming present of finite realities. It is a joy in
populating one's world with "matters" of importance. It is a joy in
the ecstasis of the self.

A meaningful community is a community of lovers, certainly not
sentimental and not necessarily erotic. Thinking and loving have a
long history of togetherness expressed explicitly in writings of Plato,
Augustine, Spinoza, Nietzsche, and others: but, also expressed in the
very word *philosophy*. *Amor fati* is a joy in reality. It is a walking in the
grove of the Furies and it is also a response to the dazzling presentation of the world in a text of love. There can be no real loving without thinking and there can be no real thinking without loving.

Index

abjection, 65, 136
absence, 1–2, 4; of Being, 24;
  presence is, in a/theology, 121;
  presence of, in theological discursive practice, 69; and topology, 129
absolute, 67; dependence, 2–5
absolute knowledge, 68, 115
abstraction, 10, 13, 67
actus purus, 114
afterthinking, 100
Agnes (in *Immortality*), 45–47, 59
Allah, 55
*Alchemy of the Word: Language and
  the End of Theology, The*
  (Raschke, Carl), 113
Altarity (Taylor, Mark C.),
  118–20
altarity, 118, 121, 124
amor amoris, 67; *fati,* 140, 150;
  intellectualis, 67
analogy, 102
animality, 37, 39
Ananke, 143
Anselm's ontological argument,
  123, 137, 146
anxiety, ix; as criterion for theolog-

ical discursive practice, 67–68;
  force and meaning of, 39; and
  temporality, 24
aporia, 74, 125
appearance(s), 19–20, 25, 36, 89;
  delight in, 118; and primary
  forces, 28–30, 39; quasi-transcendental status of, 25
apperception. *See* transcendental
  unity of apperception
arbitrariness, 45, 48, 32
Aristotle, 91, 102
art(s), 26, 91; visual, and existential phenomenology, 22
a/theology, 113–26; and theology,
  123–26
Augustine, 67, 150

Bataille, Georges, 119
becoming(s), 135, 141
beginning(s), 4, 7–8, 54; in modern philosophy, 9, 14–15
Being, beings, 89, 141; God is,
  71-74, 81; and Heidegger, 24,
  102; and theological discursive
  practice, 55-56, 101-2; and
  theological discursive practice,

paradox, 97–98; and Scharlemann, Robert P., 100–108; and
Taylor, Mark C., 120–22; topological, 85, 103, 129–30, 139;
tropological, 85, 93–4. *See also*
practice, discursive, theological;
strategy(ies); surface(s); tropology
psychoanalysis, 60
psychosis, 29

*Raid on The Articulate: Comic
Eschatology in Jesus and Borges*
(Crossan, John Dominic), 77
Raschke, Carl, 113; *The Alchemy of
the Word: Language and the End
of Theology,* 113
rationalism, 6
reading. *See* practice, discursive
real, 4, 66, 135; and important, x,
4–5, 8, 16, 25, 135; meaning of
life, 12
realism, precritical naïve, 17,
24–25
reality, 22–23, 66, 138, 141–42,
145; depth and importance, 21,
27; inner, 10; metaphor as illusion of, 33; and reason, 69; and
symbols, 74, 82; ultimate, as
wholly other, 5–6; unbearably
light, 6
reality principle, 36
reason, 46; acoluthetic, 106-11;
acoluthetic, and the Incarnation, 111-12; acoluthetic, and
tactic, 128; after Kant, 21, 25,
31; and reality, 69
referencing, intertextual, 41–42; as
deconstructive writing in Tay-

lor, Mark C., 120; as theology
for the history of religions, 66
Reformation, 114
religion(s): definitions, 4, 146-47;
history of, 14, 23; history of,
and postmodern secular theology, 65-66; institutionalized, 1-
2, 14; phenomenology of, 23;
secular studies of, 14-23
remainder, 70, 84
representation, 86–87, 89, 130,
133; and the exstantial *I,*
109–10; and the name of God,
53, 85–86
repression(s), 11, 21, 40–41, 132;
primal, 132; primal, and misreading, strong, 60; primal, and
palliatives, 145; primal, and
tropology, 18; and religion, 5–6
resonance, 41, 91
responsibility, 148
restlessness, ix, 1
Resurrection, 107, 111
reterritorialization, 135
return of the repressed, 7, 11–12,
36, 144
revelation, 5, 65, 73, 83, 102;
final, 84–85
rhetoric, 57, 90
rhizome, 15
Robbe-Grillet, Alain, 91
romanticism(s), 6–7, 10

Sabina (in *The Unbearable Lightness of Being,* Milan Kundera), 6
safety, 11, 59
salvation, 81, 83
same, 90. *See also* eternal recurrence of the same